SendPoints
est. 2006

IT'S
MY TYPE

SendPoints

IT'S MY TYPE

Second printing of the first edition, November 2019

EDITED & PUBLISHED BY SendPoints Publishing Co., Ltd.
PUBLISHER: Lin Gengli
PUBLISHING DIRECTOR: Lin Shijian
CHIEF EDITOR: Lin Shijian
EXECUTIVE EDITOR: Luo Yanmei
ART DIRECTOR: He Wanling
EXECUTIVE ART EDITOR: Peng Peng
PROOFREADING: Zhang Yu

REGISTERED ADDRESS: Room 15A Block 9 Tsui Chuk Garden, Wong Tai Sin, Kowloon, Hong Kong
TEL: +852-35832323 / **FAX:** +852-35832448
OFFICE ADDRESS: 7F, No.9-1 Anning Street, Jinshazhou Road, Baiyun District, Guangzhou, China
TEL: +86-20-89095121 / **FAX:** +86-20-89095206
BEIJING OFFICE: Flat 1701, Block C, BBMG International, Wangjing West Road no.48, Chaoyang District, Beijing, China
TEL: +86-10-84139071 / **FAX:** +86-10-84139071
SHANGHAI OFFICE: Room 302, Floor 3, Ningbo Road no.349, Huangpu District, Shanghai, China
TEL: +86-21-63523469 / **FAX:** +86-21-63523469

SALES MANAGER: Kris Guo
TEL: +86-20-81007895
EMAIL: sales@sendpoints.cn
WEBSITE: www.sendpoints.cn / www.spbooks.cn

ISBN 978-988-14704-1-6

Printed and bound in China.

Contents

TYPE MY STOR_Y

In this chapter, we feature ten type designers from different parts of the world - Canada, France, Russia, Hong Kong, and many others. Some designed Roman letters, some Cyrillic, and some Chinese. They may speak different languages, yet they share the same enthusiasm for typeface design. How did their stories begin? How is typeface design developing in their places? What are their likes and dislikes in this job? As type designers, who would they admire? And why do we need good typefaces? Let's learn about their stories and find out the answers.

Benoît Bodhuin

Gerben Dollen

Paul D. Hunt

Patrick Griffin

Raymond Larabie

Valery Golyzhenkov

Panos Vassiliou

Robin Hui

Jiying Li

Yi Ding

Benoît Bodhuin

Graphic & Type Designer
bb bureau
France

I have been designing types since 2003, when I drew a nodular font for my final study project. My favorite type designers are Gareth Hague, Emmanuel Rey, Aleš Najbrt, Jan Novák and Filip Kraus and I've certainly forgotten great others.

Typography shapes our ideas. I like the relationship between letter designs and pattern of the character string: hidden expressiveness of a single glyph disclosed by its use. Even trying to anticipate and control its behavior is always a revelation for me and the impatience of this discovery is one of the reasons that makes me love typography and motivates me to its laborious design. The only thing that I don't like about it is: designing a typeface takes a very long time!

Typography goes very well in France right now: it arouses curiosity. It is a source of experimentation, widely used as a way of expression (sometimes exclusively). And producing is very good, I think. I don't know about the future, but I guess more and more types, facilitated by type design software (like Glyphs) will become even more accessible.

Gerben Dollen

Smart Capo
Type Mafia
The Netherlands

Back in 2004, I was at a study exchange at the California College of the Arts, and attended a class by fellow dutchman Max Kisman who introduced me into typeface design, which was totally new to me. In California, I developed a love-hate relationship with type. I loved cooking up things gradually, but hated when I had to correct issues a million times. When I made a mistake, I made them everywhere, so I had to fix character after character. And of course you don't make just a single mistake but plenty instead.

In designing types, the thing that excites you is that you're creating tools (typefaces) that other people pick up and eventually you'll see your work in use by others. Not just once, but multiple times in a variety of ways and applications ranging from books to signage systems.

Are you aware of the book Dutch Type written by Jan Middendorp? In the Netherlands we have such a rich history that it's both difficult and challenging to add something new to it. Personally, I wish to see a lot more contemporary, original work. I'd like to see things I haven't seen before. I'm not much interested in revivals or something the like. So please no Garamonds and Helveticas anymore. Thanks.

Project: Istanbul Deko Designer: Istanbul Deko

Paul D. Hunt

Typeface Designer & Font Developer
Adobe
USA

I have been designing types for almost a decade now. My favourite designer is Frank Greißhammer because he is my friend. If I could marry any typeface, it would probably be Sauna by Underware.

We need good typefaces for the same reason as we need anything that is well-designed — to inject more beauty into our lives. Reading is a big part of interfacing with ideas and concepts and that process should be as comfortable and enjoyable as possible. Pleasing typefaces allow us to focus more intently on the content of a message and less on the form.

Luckily, there is a plethora of well-designed typefaces available for Latin script. I feel really blessed to have those varieties available to me. However, I find that because of the proliferation and ease of use of good type, it is harder and harder to find good hand lettering in public places. I hope that lettering will make more of a return in America in the future.

Patrick Griffin

Type Director
Canada Type
Canada

Type design is something I've always liked to do. At a young age I was fascinated by type as a vessel that delivers the message to the reader, and how the method of delivery affects the perception of the message itself. So I decided to focus my attention on that particular dynamic, and that was the beginning of the journey. Up to now, I have been doing this all in all for something like 28 years.

Typeface is the medium in which the content is delivered, so there's a direct correlation there: If you don't use an appropriate face for your content, you are indicating that you have little respect for your message — and that lack of respect makes its way to the reader.

In Canada, there are plenty of typefaces by very good type designers, and more typefaces are being produced on a regular basis. As far as I am concerned, type designers in general are supposed to be direct tool suppliers to graphic designers and communicators, but too much middle management is complicating that relationship. If I could make one change in the industry, it would be to shave off at least one layer of bureaucracy.

Project: Type Directors Club Annual Exhibition in Taiwan 2014 Designer: ken-tsai Lee

Raymond Larabie

Head Honcho
Typodermic Fonts Inc.
Japan

When I was about 5 years old, my grandmother would bring me partially used dry-transfer lettering sheets and type catalogs from work. I got really obsessed with letterforms and identifying fonts by name. I've always been a fan of Microgramma by Aldo Novarese; it is the Alpha and the Omega of techno fonts.

As a Canadian living in Japan, I don't even bother making Japanese typefaces because I don't have the time, knowledge or resources. With a collection of 80,000 Japanese characters, I'd need to take a couple of years to work on one. In Japan, font sales are totally different from what I'm used to. They're usually sold in collections, not as individual font licenses.

Typefaces are art supplies. You can make do with limited, poor quality art supplies. But you're making more work for yourself and the end result might not be as good. I also think the fonts a designer chooses say something about themselves. If you stick with the classics, you might do great work but it might reveal that you're afraid to take risks.

Valery Golyzhenkov

letterhead studio
Russia

I don't consider myself a type designer. The more accurate definition would be this: I am a graphic designer with experience in type design. Why? Often I find myself in a situation, where there is no ready-made solutions for my design, or there is no Cyrillic version of the fonts I need. And it seems that there is no chance of getting them, unless I do it myself. But, thank God, that's when I know exactly what to do.

In Russia there is an enormous interest in type design. Every year more and more people are willing to put their efforts in this area. Around 50 trained type design specialists graduate every year, and you can add to this a decent number of self-taught amateurs. We get more and more Cyrillic typefaces, and yet we still are in shortage.

We need more good typefaces. Because they help the communication; that's the most important part. A good typeface, alongside with good typography can deliver more than just information. The only problem is how we can distinguish a good typeface. I, for one, think that fonts from forhomeorofficeuse.com are very good, but how many people are going to agree with me on it?

一壶茶 清润晶透 幽香萦绕 味在舌尖 意远千里
此刻 与久违的自己在此相遇 以最慵散的姿态 让思绪盛放
悠悠然 独享这份清风雨露
滚烫的水 生出浓郁的烟 好时光 慢慢品

Project: Chinese Tea Identity Designer: Pang Guoping

Panos Vassiliou

Type Designer
Parachute
Greece

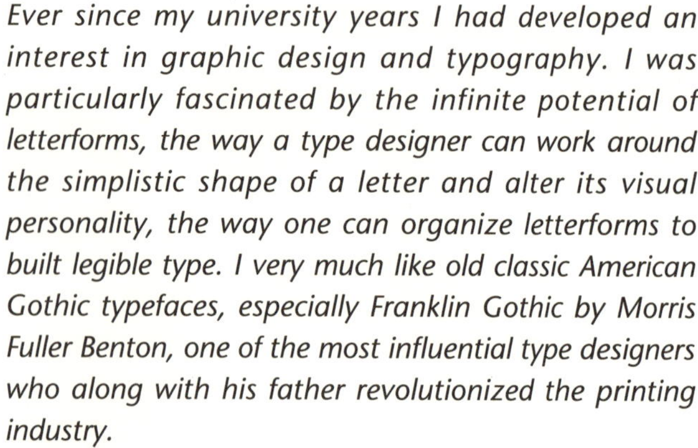

Ever since my university years I had developed an interest in graphic design and typography. I was particularly fascinated by the infinite potential of letterforms, the way a type designer can work around the simplistic shape of a letter and alter its visual personality, the way one can organize letterforms to built legible type. I very much like old classic American Gothic typefaces, especially Franklin Gothic by Morris Fuller Benton, one of the most influential type designers who along with his father revolutionized the printing industry.

Good type design is an attempt to achieve the perfect balance between geometric perfection and optical perfection, a balance between our rational mind and our free-spirited artistic nature. It is exactly this attempt to achieve a visual balance using the rational modular shapes of the alphabet that drives me and excites me during the designing process.

We don't just need good typefaces; we need typefaces that communicate better, typefaces that offer real market solutions, typefaces that sell products, typefaces that reflect local market trends and culture. There are already too many commercial fonts in the market. It is time for companies to seek bespoke solutions if they want to differentiate themselves from competitors.

Robin Hui

Chief Designer & Production Manager
Monotype Hong Kong Limited
Hong Kong

Back when I was a kid, my dad would ask my sister to write red couplets during spring festivals because her handwriting was the best in the family. How envious I was that dad was in favor of her! I have since been interested in good handwritings and typefaces. Up to now, I have been designing types for almost 30 years. My favourite type designer is Adrian Frutiger who dedicated his whole life to type design. My favourite typefaces are Frutiger and M Sung by Monotype.

Developing Western and Chinese typefaces are very different — an individual can handle the former quite well; despite similar design work, production of the latter requires team work because of its enormous character set. I feel satisfied when a team is working together contributing to and creating an impact on history. What I do not like is when I have to compromise art with business.

Ideographic characters in different places of the Asia-Pacific region are written slightly differently. To develop consistency in a global font requires designers from different places to work and solve these problems together. As far as I can see, technology very much governs how fonts are used and the future of our industry. Also, technology itself continues to play an important role in how fonts are developed.

Project: ¡Mestizo Designer: Melville Brand Design

Jiying Li

Type Director
Arphic Technology co., Ltd.
Taiwan

Yi Ding

Type Designer and Founder
Make Font
China

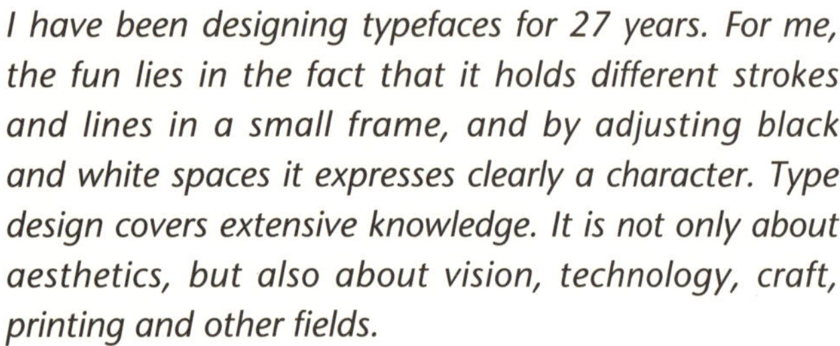

I have been designing typefaces for 27 years. For me, the fun lies in the fact that it holds different strokes and lines in a small frame, and by adjusting black and white spaces it expresses clearly a character. Type design covers extensive knowledge. It is not only about aesthetics, but also about vision, technology, craft, printing and other fields.

With so many Chinese characters and all those complicated strokes and structures, it takes a long time to develop and it requires patience, perseverance and team work. While developing Chinese fonts is difficult, font users, on the other hand, are not aware enough of the fact that they should actually pay for using fonts. This makes it even more difficult for the industry to grow. Only when the industry gains the equal value from the market will talents and resources continously enrich it.

Interest is the best teacher. I have always been interested in all kinds of Chinese handwritings, and now as a type designer I hope to do something for Chinese typefaces. I love these famous Japanese designers, Yoshimaru Takahashi, Sugiura Kohei and Katsumi Asaba. They have very wise and sharp insights into Hanzi. Akira Kobayashi, Isao Suzuki and Osamu Torinoumi have different styles for typefaces; their works look different and are applied under different visual environments.

People love seeing beautiful things, because it's a spiritual enjoyment. There's no right or wrong, pretty or ugly typeface. Typefaces themselves are like costumes, which are made for different roles and different sets. It is the best only when it fits.

Currently, we can see and use numerous Western fonts. But for Chinese characters, the intellectual property right does not receive enough respect, and for that not many people are willing to work in this field, which makes it harder for the industry to develop. It deserves respect and I hope that people can stop using it for commercial purpose without authorization, so that it can survive and thrive.

abcdef

ghijkl

mnopq

rstuv

wxyz

Project: Vetka type Designer: Ruslan Khasanov

TYPEFACE STYLE AND APPLICATION

90 Artistic Typeface

1

Typeface in Branding

Handcrafted News Gothic regular

ABCDEFGHI
JKLMNOPQR
STUVWXYZ
ÆØÅÄ

Feldthusen

Studio: mousegraphics

To better adjust to different uses for small and large quantities, designers assembled an original, recognizable and flexible visual tool: a new letter type, a custom made, hand over-painted, organic looking version of News Gothic MT.

Essem Design

Designer: Mattias Amnäs
Studio: Bedow

This is a design of product catalogue for Essem Design, a Swedish manufacturer of artisanal hallway interior. The concept "Hej—Hej då" (Hello—Goodbye) refers to the most common phrase in the hallway.

The hallway is the architect's way of saying hello and goodbye

Essem
Design

Swedish manufacturer
of artisanal hallway interior

Sten-Roger Bladh, VD
+46 (0)706 19 41 06
srb@essem.se
www.essem.se

Essem
Design

Swedish manufacturer
of artisanal hallway interior

Essem Design
Hantverkargatan 36
334 31 Anderstorp, Sweden
+46 (0)371 194 10
info@essem.se
www.essem.se

Gloria
by Joel Karlsson

122

122

66

Gloria

When Joel Karlsson got the assignment to design a new hook, he reflected on how to complement the traditional coat hook to better accomodate garments without a hanger. "We wanted to create a product that 'forgives' the garment the same way a hanger does," says Karlsson about his innovative hook provided with a halo.

Description and Measurements

The hook is moulded in recycled aluminium and powder coated. Gloria measures 122x66x122mm (WxDxH) and is delivered with the necessary screws in a box.

Designs

Art. no 170-0	Black structure(9005*)
Art. no 170-00	Black(9005)
Art. no 170-1	Traffic blue(5017)
Art. no 170-15	Bordeaux violet (4004)
Art. no 170-2	Zinc yellow(1018)
Art. no 170-3	Red orange(2004)
Art. no 170-4	Traffic red(3020)
Art. no 170-46	Pink(4003)
Art. no 170-5	Spearmint green(6029)
Art. no 170-53	Yellow green(6018)
Art. no 170-55	Light green (turquoise)(6018)
Art. no 170-8	Traffic white(9016)
Art. no 170-9	Aluminum nature
Art. no 170-99	Silver

*RAL no

Essem
Design

Swedish manufacturer
of artisanal hallway interior

Essem Design
Hantverkargatan 36
334 31 Anderstorp, Sweden
+46 (0)371 194 10
info@essem.se
www.essem.se

Nostalgi
by Gunnar Bohlin

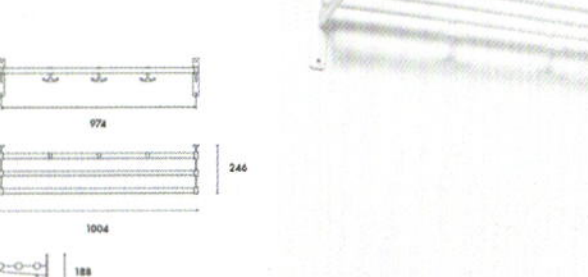

976

246

1004

188

Nostalgi

Gunnar Bohlin designed the hat and shoe rack Nostalgi in 1937. The rack has come and gone through the decades, but is today a classic in Swedish furniture history. The consoles are manufactured, as they've always been, by melted aluminium scrap and are joined with wooden staffs.

Description and Measurements

Nostalgi has consoles and anchor hooks in moulded recycled aluminium. The wooden shelves are dowels made of birch, beech or oak. The shelves are also available in powder coated or chromed steel pipes or naturally anodized aluminium pipes. The baseline measure is 1000x245x190mm (WxDxH), but the width can either be extended by adding an additional part* or reduced by cutting off a part. The shelf is delivered disassembled in a box.

Designs

Art. no 001	Beech / Black
Art. no 003	Black / Black
Art. no 006	Beech / Alu
Art. no 009	Black / Alu
Art. no 010	Alu/Alu
Art. no 015	Birch / Black
Art. no 017	Birch / Alu
Art. no 019	Oak / Black
Art. no 021	Oak / Alu
Art. no 023	Chrome / Black
Art. no 025	Chrome / Alu
Art. no 027	Alu / Black

A. Amigos del Malba®.

Designer: Nicolás Vasino
Studio: Empatía®

The designer sought the highest possible quality of typeface design down to the last detail, making it long lasting, environmental, and economically as well as socially sustainable, with the belief of " back to purity, back to simplicity".

gura-
2013
seo de
ericano
es.
ntrada.

Joven.

Friendship.
Art.
Museum.
Young.

éfono. +54 4808-6511 / 6513—Avenida Figueroa
corta 3415, CABA, Buenos Aires, Argentina.
ociación@malba.org.ar—amigos@malba.org.ar

Amigos
de
Malba®.

Ford Ka

Typography & Lettering: Rutger Paulusse (gwer)
Concept & Art Direction: Bas Derks
Agency: Ogilvy Amsterdam
Agent: Artbox

The designer created 30 customized "word images" for the Ford Ka campaign. Every word has its own characteristics so that its visual presentation meets the meaning of the word.

MODERN SPORTIEF vriendelijk

Sexy creatief Flexibel

ENTHOUSIAST Extravagant NUCHTER

SNEL Optimistisch Pittig

Lief SPONTAAN Brutaal

TROUW AMBITIEUS eigenwijs

-STOER- UITDAGEND vrolijk

SOCIAAL AVONTUURLIJK EXPRESSIEF

S·P·E·E·L·S ondeugend Relaxed

Gevoelig bescheiden KRACHTIG

Mexout

Designer: Jasmine Lee
Studio: Bravo

Being anti-establishment, Mexout doesn't adopt only one certain brand logo. Every time you see the brand it appears differently. 20 hand-drawn logos are used in rotation.

MEXOUT

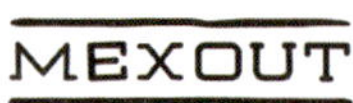

YOU ARE WHAT YOU EAT. SO I AM TACO
MEXOUT
MEXOUT

LIFE'S LIKE A BURRITO. YOU HAVE TO FILL IT UP WITH THE BEST INGREDIENTS.
MEXOUT
MEXOUT
39 PEKIN STREET
FAR EAST SQUARE
S'PORE 048769
T: +65 9770 7441
WWW.MEXOUT.COM
OPENS LUNCH
& DINNER

MAKE SALSA NOT WAR.
MEXOUT
THE TACO CANNON
MEXOUT

Mexout

MEXOUT

MEXOUT

Commonwealth

Designer: Jennifer Lucey-Brzoza
Studio: Oat

Commonwealth is a restaurant and urban food market rooted in Vermont farm life. The identity and packaging draws on the human touch of billboards painted on roadside barns and canned preserves labeled by a neighbor's hand. The print materials evoke the charms of seed catalogs and feedbags of the 1940's.

Market
COMMONWEALTH
CAMBRIDGE

CW
PINK PEARL
WINESAP
WINTER HARDY

FINEST PICKLING
CUCUMBERS
- MUNCHER -
CW

CW

COMMONWEALTH
EAT
GOOD
FOOD
CW

COCKTAILS
CLASSIC COCKTAILS
COMMONWEALTH CLASSICS
CHEESY CLASSICS
NEGRONI
Gin, Sweet Vermouth, Campari
$10
NOOKIE
Gin, Mint Simple, Lime Juice
$10
WHITE RUSSIAN
House Made Espresso Liquor, Vodka, Creami
$10
TOM COLLINS
Gin, Lemon, Simple, Soda
$10
THE CHARLES
Rum, Maschino Liquor, Cherry Simple, Averna Mole Bitters
$12
SEX ON THE BEACH
Vodka, Peach Liquor, Grenadine, OJ
$11
RAMOS GIN FIZZ
Gin, Lemon, Orange Flower Water, Simple, Cream, Egg White
$10
SEASONAL MILK PUNCH
Secret
$12
PEAL HARBOR
Tequila, Pineapple Juice, Melon Liquor
$12
VIEUX CARRE
Rye, Cognac, Lemon, Sweet Vermouth, Benedictine, Paychaud Bitters, Angostura Bitters
$10
DIRTY WATER
Tequila, Spicy Simple, Grapefruit Juice, Lime Juice, Orange Juice, Grenadine
$12
APPLE MARTINI
Granny Smith Apple Liquor, Apple Vodka, Sparkling Cider
$12
DAIQUIRI
Rum, Lime Juice, Simple Syrup
$10
GIN SOUR
Gin, Green Chartreause, Lime Juice, Simple, Egg White
$12
AMARETTO SOUR
Luxardo Amaretto, Cherry Liquor, Lemon Juice
$11
OLD FASHIONED
Bourbon, Angostura Bitters, Sugar
$10
SWEET, SALTY & SMOKEY
Mescal, Sweet Vermouth, Bitters, Simple, Kosher Salt
$12
WOO WOO
Citrus Vodka, Cherry Heering, Peach Liquor, Cranberry Juice
$11
SIDECAR
Brandy, Orange Liquor, Lemon Juice
$10
THE CANAL
Rye, Averna, Chery Heering, Lemon Juice, Mole Bitters
$12
$0

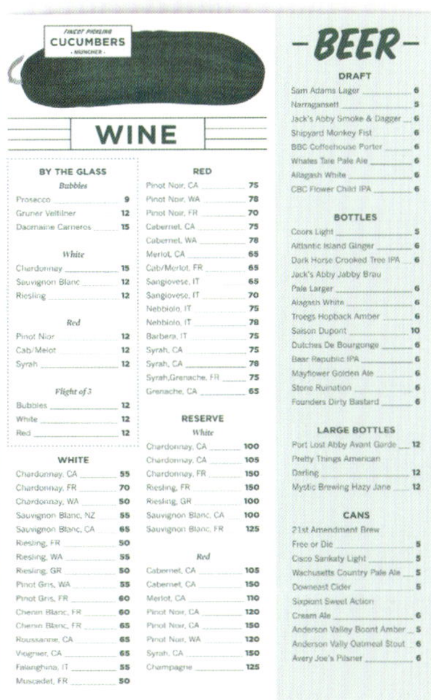
CUCUMBERS
WINE
BY THE GLASS
Bubbles
Prosecco 9
Gruner Veltilner 12
Daomaine Carneros 15
White
Chardonney 15
Sauvignon Blanc 12
Riesling 12
Red
Pinot Nior 12
Cab/Meiot 12
Syrah 12
Flight of 3
Bubbles 12
White 12
Red 12
RED
Pinot Noir, CA 75
Pinot Noir, WA 78
Pinot Noir, FR 70
Cabernet, CA 75
Cabernet, WA 78
Merlot, CA 65
Cab/Merlot, FR 65
Sangiovese, IT 65
Sangiovese, IT 70
Nebbiolo, IT 75
Nebbiolo, IT 78
Barbera, IT 75
Syrah, CA 75
Syrah, CA 78
Syrah,Grenache, FR 75
Grenache, CA 65
WHITE
Chardonnay, CA 55
Chardonnay, FR 70
Chardonnay, WA 50
Sauvignon Blanc, NZ 55
Sauvignon Blanc, CA 65
Riesling, FR 50
Riesling, WA 55
Riesling, GR 50
Pinot Gris, WA 55
Pinot Gris, FR 60
Chenin Blanc, FR 60
Chenin Blanc, FR 65
Roussanne, CA 65
Viognier, CA 65
Falanghina, IT 55
Muscadet, FR 50
RESERVE
White
Chardonnay, CA 100
Chardonnay, CA 105
Chardonnay, FR 150
Riesling, FR 150
Riesling, GR 100
Sauvignon Blanc, CA 100
Sauvignon Blanc, FR 125
Red
Cabernet, CA 105
Cabernet, CA 150
Merlot, CA 110
Pinot Noir, CA 120
Pinot Noir, CA 150
Pinot Noir, WA 120
Syrah, CA 150
Champagne 125
BEER
DRAFT
Sam Adams Lager 6
Narragansett 5
Jack's Abby Smoke & Dagger 6
Shipyard Monkey Fist 6
BBC Coffeehouse Porter 6
Whales Tale Pale Ale 6
Allagash White 6
CBC Flower Child IPA 6
BOTTLES
Coors Light 5
Atlantic Island Ginger 6
Dark Horse Crooked Tree IPA 6
Jack's Abby Jabby Brau
Pale Larger 6
Alagash White 6
Troegs Hopback Amber 6
Saison Dupont 10
Dutches De Bourgonge 6
Bear Republic IPA 6
Mayflower Golden Ale 6
Stone Ruination 6
Founders Dirty Bastard 6
LARGE BOTTLES
Port Lost Abby Avant Garde 12
Pretty Things American Darling 12
Mystic Brewing Hazy Jane 12
CANS
21st Amendment Brew
Free or Die 5
Cisco Sankaty Light 5
Wachusetts Country Pale Ale 5
Downeast Cider 5
Sixpoint Sweet Action
Cream Ale 6
Anderson Valley Boont Amber 5
Anderson Vally Oatmeal Stout 6
Avery Joe's Pilsner 6

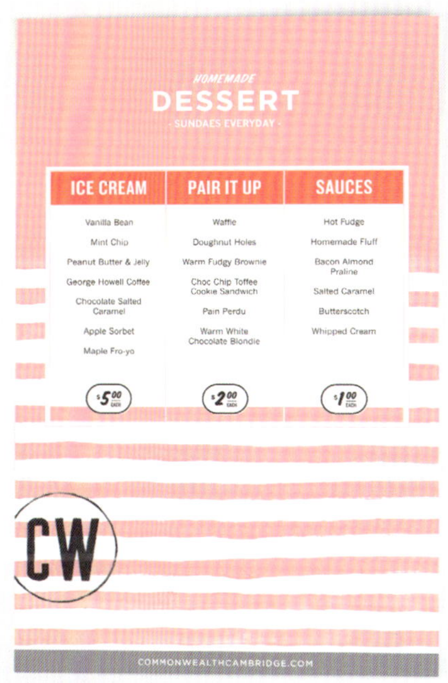
HOMEMADE
DESSERT
- SUNDAES EVERYDAY -
ICE CREAM
Vanilla Bean
Mint Chip
Peanut Butter & Jelly
George Howell Coffee
Chocolate Salted Caramel
Apple Sorbet
Maple Fro-yo
$5.00 EACH
PAIR IT UP
Waffle
Doughnut Holes
Warm Fudgy Brownie
Choc Chip Toffee Cookie Sandwich
Pain Perdu
Warm White Chocolate Blondie
$2.00 EACH
SAUCES
Hot Fudge
Homemade Fluff
Bacon Almond Praline
Salted Caramel
Butterscotch
Whipped Cream
$1.00 EACH
CW
COMMONWEALTHCAMBRIDGE.COM

L'ingredient Identity

Designer: Núria Vila & Albert Grèbol
Studio: Can Cun

L'ingredient is a little shop in Manresa. To show that the shop is a place where people can shop conveniently, a Monosten typeface from the studio The Entente, which is stenciled, rounded and mono-spaced, is used to identify the brand.

Tenim molt
bé de preu:
Ametlla
marcona
crua
2,18 €/ 100 gr
Curs
bàsic
de cuina
natural
0g de farina
0g de sucre
g de llevat
0g de mantega
0ml de llet
llimona/taronja
igua d'azahar
ou i sal
ORTELL DE REIS
CIGRÓ PETIT

Karl-Jonas & Blood Music

Designer: Mattias Amnäs
Studio: Bedow

This is a record sleeve for The Light of the Future (Dark of the Past) album by Swedish artist Karl Jonas & Blood Music and was released on the Sing a Song Fighter label.

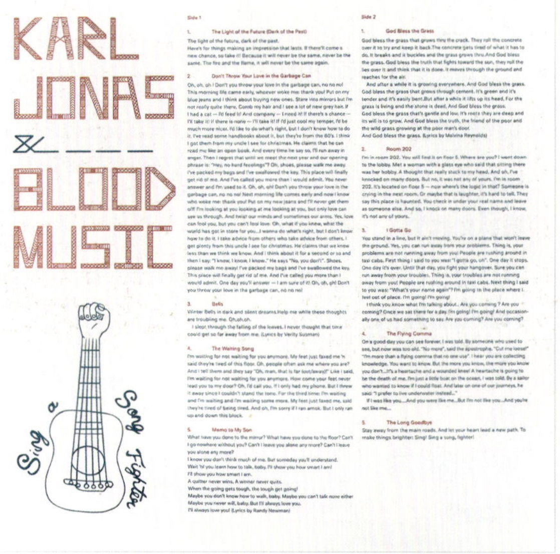

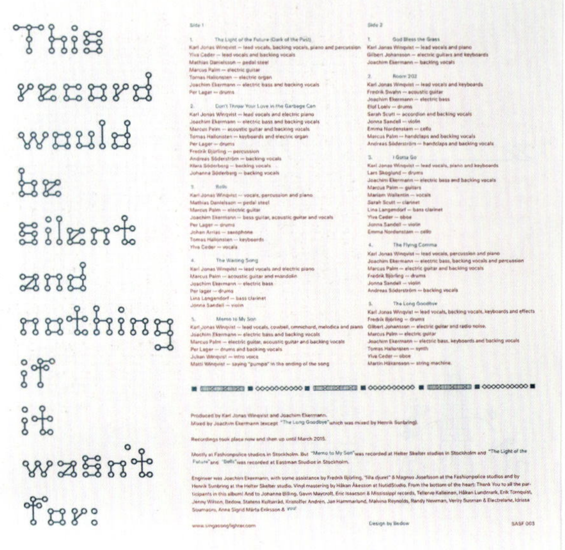

KARL
JONAS
&
BLOOD
MUSIC
The Light of the Future
Dark of the Past

KARL JONAS
&
BLOOD MUSIC
Side one
The Light of the Future
Dark of the Past

Side two
Side one
01. The Light of the Future
Dark of the Past
02. Don't Throw Your Love
in the Garbage Can
03. Bells
04. The Waiting Song
05. Memo to My Son
Side two
01. God Bless the Grass
02. I Gotta Go
03. Room 202
04. The Flying Comma
05. The Long Goodbye
157 /300

Design Terminal Identity and Signage

Designer: kissmiklos
Photographer: Bálint Jaksa

Design Terminal is an agency for creative industries in Budapest, Hungary. They promote the development of the creative industries. This typeface corresponds to the historical building by applying the style of old neon signs from the 50's, while maintaining a unique, interesting, suggestive and playful futuristic sense.

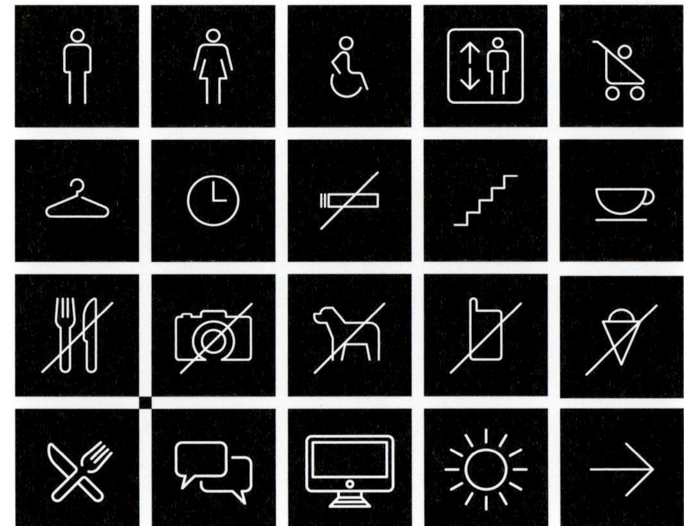

ÁCS ZOLTÁN

Creative director
Kreatív igazgató

Telefon/fax: 00 36 1 327 7208 / 00 36 1 327 7209
Mobil: 00 36 30 241 2213
Email: zoltan.acs@designterminal.hu

1051 Budapest, Erzsébet tér 13.
www.designterminal.hu

Kreatív igazgató / creative director

Telefon:
00 36 1 327 7208
Fax:
00 36 1 327 7209
Mobil:
00 36 30 241 2213
Email:
zoltan.acs@designterminal.hu

1051 Budapest, Erzsébet tér 13.
www.designterminal.hu

NŐI / WOMEN
FÉRFI / MEN

TECHNOLOGY
DESIGN
FASHION
URBANISM

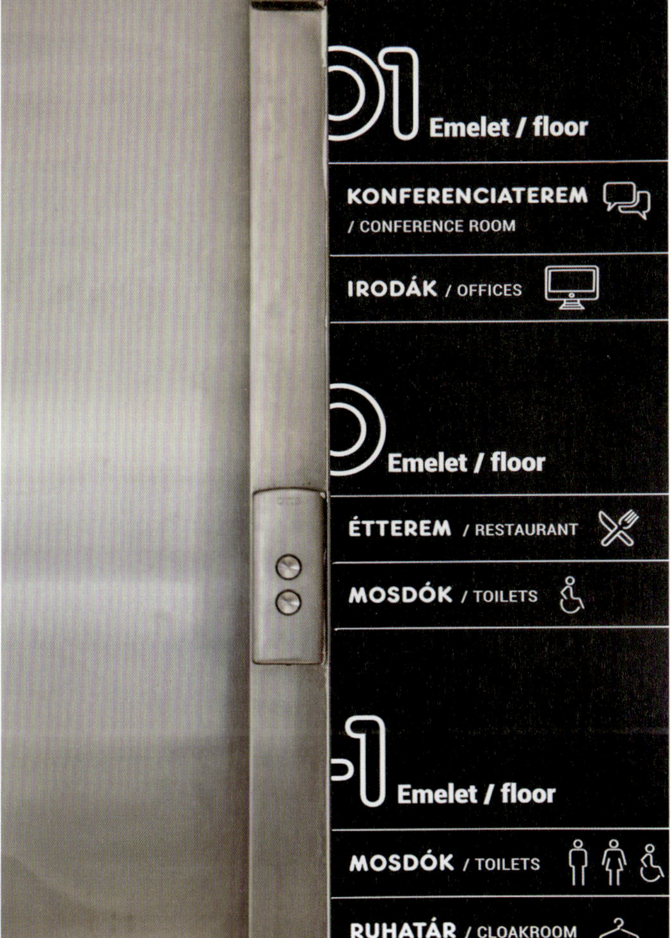
01 Emelet / floor
KONFERENCIATEREM / CONFERENCE ROOM
IRODÁK / OFFICES
0 Emelet / floor
ÉTTEREM / RESTAURANT
MOSDÓK / TOILETS
-1 Emelet / floor
MOSDÓK / TOILETS
RUHATÁR / CLOAKROOM

DESIGN
TERMINAL
IRODÁK

DESIGN TERMINAL

DESIGN TERMINAL
TERMINAL
TERMINAL

TERASZ TERRACE
IRODÁK OFFICES

Monte Xanic

Studio: Anagrama

Monte Xanic is a Mexican winery operating since 1989. The proposed icon for this project bolsters the concept of Monte Xanic (which translates into: "Flower born after the first rain"). The icon presents a flower, a drop and a crown of parra leaves. The typographic treatment evokes a sense of contemporary belonging to a brand that already denoted tradition and experience.

MONTE XANIC

BODEGA VINÍCOLA

CATÁLOGO

VINOS Y VARIADEDES

CONTACTO

MONTE XANIC

MENÚ DE DEGUSTACIONES

JAMES FOSBURG 01

CEO

montexanic.com.mx @Monte_Xanic

MONTE XANIC

BODEGA VINÍCOLA

MONTE XANIC

BODEGA VINÍCOLA

MONTEXANIC.COM.MX

VINÍCOLA

@Monte_Xanic

MONTE XANIC

BODEGA VINÍCOLA

Anchor Down

Art Directors: Scott Hill, Travis Ladue
Photographer: Judson Copeland
Studio: Studio Mast

Keeping with the industrial theme of the storage container where they set up the shop, the brand is bright, bold, and eager to never take itself too seriously. A combination of traditional industrial style, heavy inspiration from WPA posters, and sarcastic copywriting leads to a loud and sometimes goofy tone for the restaurant's brand.

4
2
ANCHOR DOWN

A/D

RESTROOMS
ARE THAT-A-WAY

FIGHT ON
FLY OKC
SUPPORT

Crossfit Collingwood

Designer: Nebojsa Matkovic
Studio: Full Moon Design

Crossfit is positioned as an audacious sport program. Therefore, the designer was trying to communicate a strong, simple and bold sense by adding dirt textures to wear off straight and thick lines so that it looked raw and hard-core.

FINISH WITH NO REGRETS

IT NEVER GETS EASIER...
YOU GET STRONGER

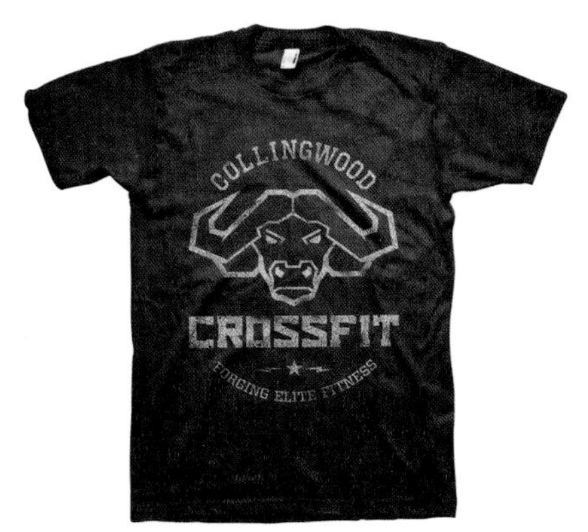
COLLINGWOOD
CROSSFIT
FORGING ELITE FITNESS

CROSSFIT

AS
STRONG
AS AN
OX

COLLINGWOOD
CROSSFIT
FORGING ELITE FITNESS
Joshua Hromis
Head Coach
75 Cromwell Street
Collingwood VIC 3066

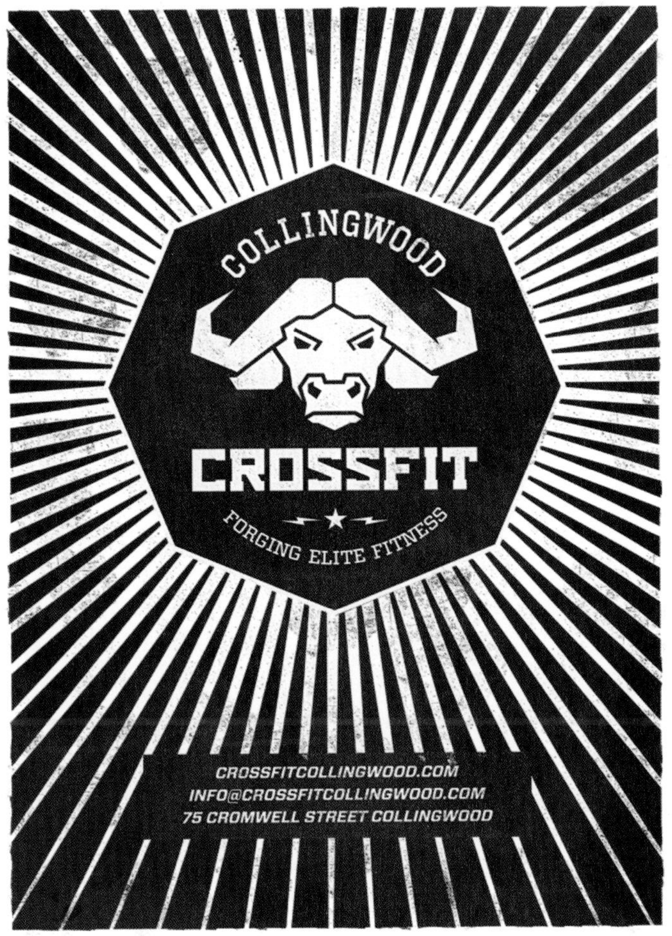
COLLINGWOOD
CROSSFIT
FORGING ELITE FITNESS
CROSSFITCOLLINGWOOD.COM
INFO@CROSSFITCOLLINGWOOD.COM
75 CROMWELL STREET COLLINGWOOD

CROSSFIT
COLLINGWOOD
WHAT IS IT?
CONSTANTLY VARIED
(Different every session)
FUNCTIONAL MOVEMENT
(How we move in real life)
HIGH INTENSITY
(Heart rate goes north)
WE START HERE →
SPORT
WEIGHTLIFTING & THROWING
GYMNASTICS
METABOLIC CONDITIONING
NUTRITION
AND BY USING THIS
NEUROLOGICAL FITNESS
Balance
Coordination
Agility
Accuracy
PHYSICAL SKILLS
Strength
Flexibility
Endurance
Stamina
WE ADD IT TO THIS:
BY USING A COMBINATION OF WEIGHTLIFTING, GYMNASTICS,RUNNING & ROWING, WHICH IS ALL SCALED TO SUIT YOUR LEVEL OF ABILITY
ESSENCE OF FITNESS
POWER + SPEED
AND THEN BY:
× FOLLOWING THE WOD'S
× DEVELOPING YOUR SKILLS
× EATING WELL
× WORKING ON YOUR MOBILITY
IT GETS US:
INCREASED WORK CAPACITY
OVER BROAD TIME & MODAL DOMAINS
WHICH MEANS!
WE CAN DO MORE IN ANY AMOUNT OF TIME AT ANYTHING WE WANT TO DO
"REAL FITNESS"

Brass

Designer: Jennifer Lucey-Brzoza
Studio: Oat

Metallic ink, official seals and document stamps send the message that the top brass expect protocol to be followed, even after they knock off. Menu backs appropriate the material and aesthetic of etched plastic municipal signage. The naming and copywriting imbue the project with a firm sense of place, celebrating Somerville and its proud 'Villens'.

SOMERVILLENS
SOME AREN'T

BRASS
UNION

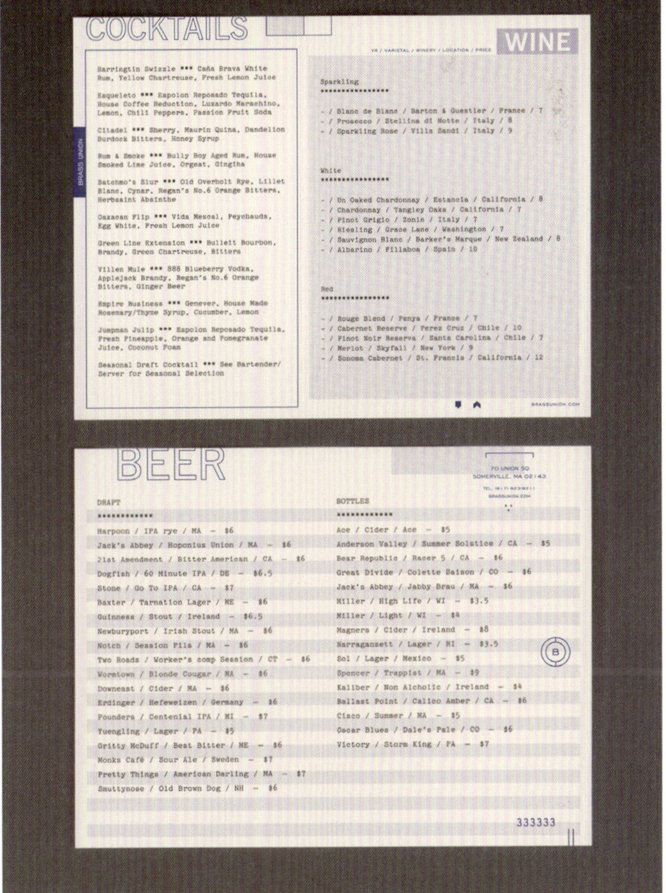

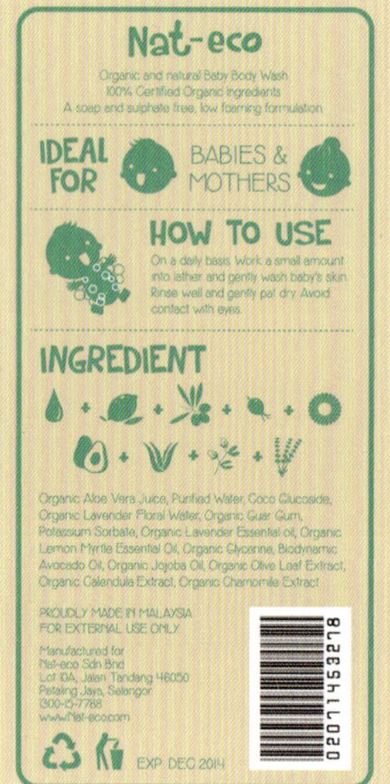

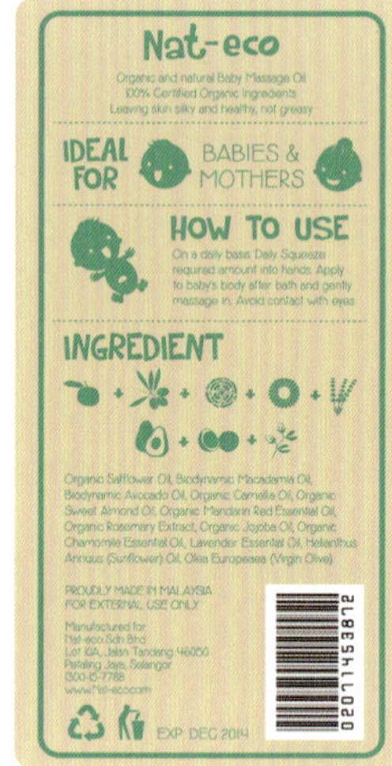

Nat-eco Baby Product

Designer: Czee Cheong

The typography is designed to convey the belief that it is guaranteed 100% pure and safe for babies and mothers. So the tone and manners are natural, organic and safe with the application of green color and playful shapes in typography.

BABY SHAMPOO

BABY MOISTURISER/ MASSAGE OIL

BABY BODY WASH

Nat-eco
Yes! It's a 100% ORGANIC BABY SHAMPOO
Nat-eco
Yes! It's a 100% ORGANIC BABY BODY WASH
Nat-eco
Yes! It's a 100% ORGANIC BABY SOAP
Nat-eco
IDEAL FOR
BABIES & MOTHERS
HOW TO USE
INGREDIENT
Nat-eco
Yes! It's a 100% ORGANIC BABY MASSAGE OIL

Nat-eco

Pereg QRC

Designer: Guillaume Federighi
Studio: SQUAT DESIGN

Each package was artistically designed with customized hand-made calligraphy. The result was tasteful packages that stimulate consumers and visually communicate a product that is healthy and wholesome.

2D – Port Wine Cocktails

Designer: Catarina Antunes e Hugo Silva
Studio: SOMA Design Studio

While '2D' reminds us of the old era, the main goal of this typeface is to create a new impression and a new way to think of the past and to reinvent a young, retro and trendy feeling towards the brand.

6 CL DE PORTO
BRANCO
4 gomos
DE LIMA
2 CL DE XAROPE DE AÇÚCAR
(ou 2 colheres de açúcar em pó)
GELO PICADO

CAIPIPORTO
COCKTAIL
BRANCO

ROSÉ
2D
BRANCO &
ROSÉ

2D
BRANCO &
ROSÉ

2D
BRANCO &
ROSÉ

LIVRO
de
COCKTAILS
2D
BRANCO &
ROSÉ
2 DIMENSÕES DE SABOR

8 MAI
BAIRRO
ALTO
20H
2D
BRANCO &
ROSÉ
2 DIMENSÕES DE SABOR

Designer: Koh Min Yu

FIVE is a box set aims to enable readers to have an interactive experience while learning more about themselves through the 10 different types of divination available. The typefaces used and created are predominately serifs to better showcase the elegance and subtlety of the ancient art of divination.

馬
HORSE
猴
MONKEY
蛇
SNAKE
龍
DRAGON
豬
PIG
兔
RABBIT
羊
GOAT
鼠
RAT
雞
ROOSTER
狗
DOG

Personal Stationery

Designer: Josh Nychuk
Studio: Nychuk Design

Nychuk Design tended to articulate the classic business-like calmness by using black, gray and white and took advantage of a production method in which a middle layer containing contact information was laser-cut and sandwiched between two outer sheets of paper to balance the calmness with playfulness.

nychuk
design/
photo-
graphy
Josh Nychuk
+1 604 837 2496
josh@nychukdesign.com
nychukdesign.com
to/
from/
Nychuk Design
102–321 Railway Street
Vancouver, BC, V6A 1A4

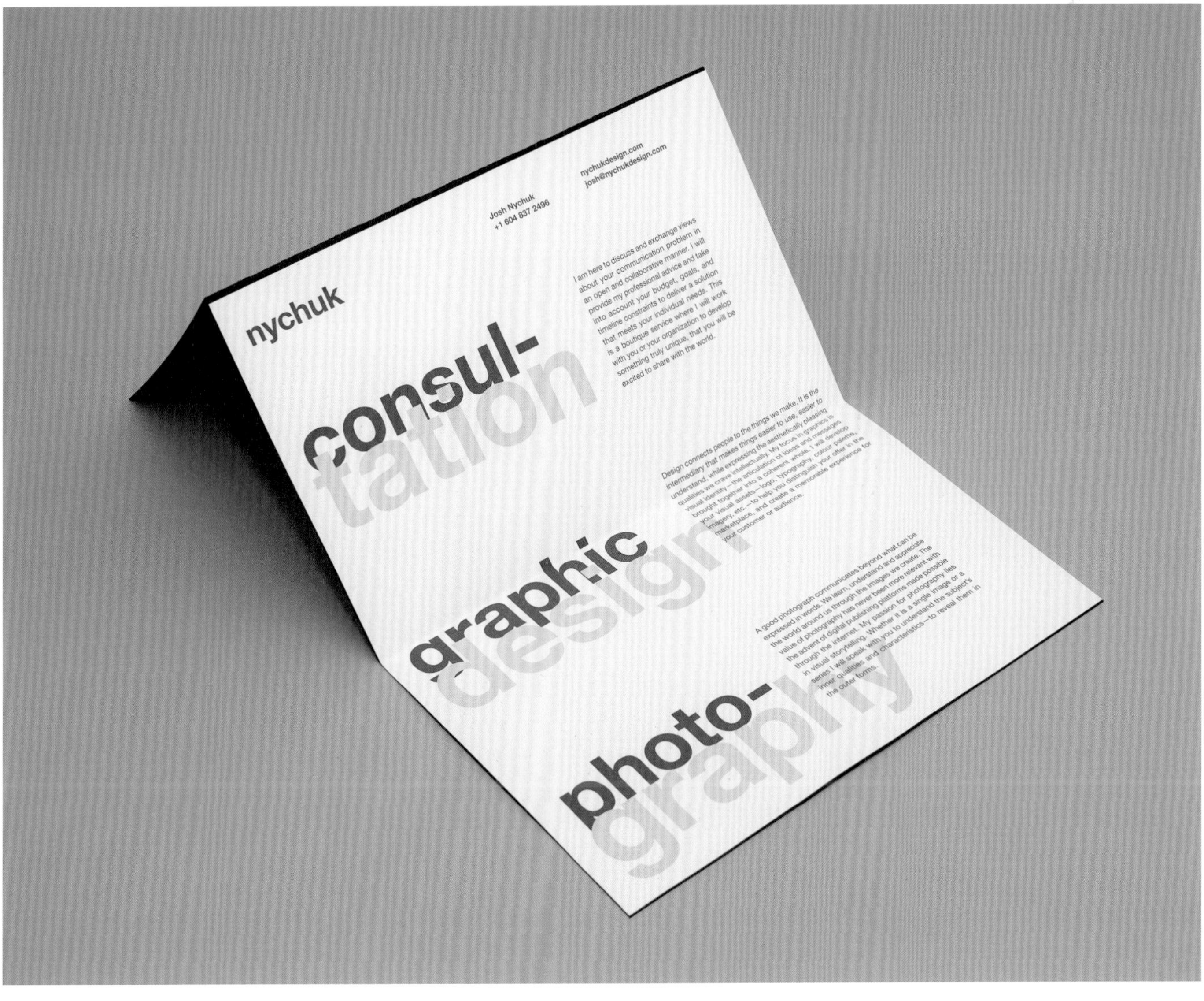

Macanudo

Studio: Lisboa Estudio Creativo

To give an impression of relaxation and vintage, the typeface design was created in a way that can not only fit in with khaki, navy blue and glory red, but is also fluid in a playful shape inspired by a variety of music and drinks the bar provides.

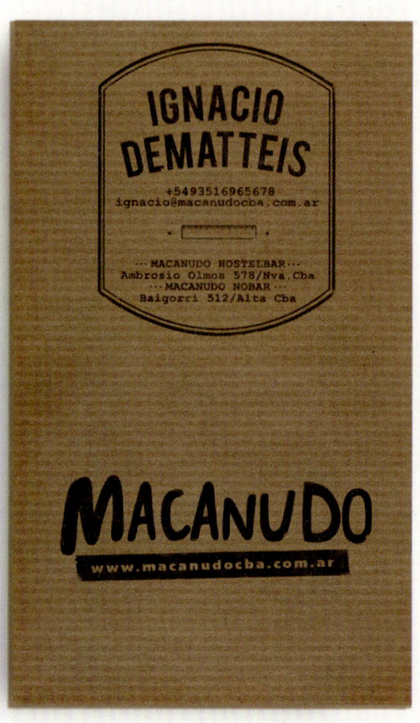

MACANUDO
HOSTELBAR

PRESENTA

Meriendas de DOMINGO

MUSICALIZA
SONIDOS RECIÉN HORNEADOS

OMRV 4tet

13 DE OCTUBRE
18:00 HORAS

MACANUDO
HOSTELBAR
Ambrosio Olmos 578

BOLSA
MACA-
-NUDA

SOMOS UN HOSTELBAR
MACANUDO
HOSTELBAR
NO SOMOS UN HOSTEL
ORIGEN.
CÓRDOBA / ARGENTINA
BUSCANOS.
WWW.MACANUDOCBA.COM.AR

SOMOS UN HOSTELBAR
MACANUDO
HOSTELBAR
NO SOMOS UN HOSTEL
ORIGEN.
CÓRDOBA / ARGENTINA
BUSCANOS.
WWW.MACANUDOCBA.COM.AR

CAFÉ &
SOUP

MACANUDO

MANGI Y CHUPÍ
PER TU. TTÌ
(COMIDA ITALIANA)
PASTA QUESOS ENSALADAS
CRUDITES ACEITUNAS
SANDWICHES
PIZZAS
MACANUDO NOBAR
CYNAR CAMPARI CINZANO
JUEVES 05.09.13

Coca-Cola Tet 2014

Designers: Nguyen Huynh, Hai Nguyen, Truc Dinh
Studio: Rice Creative

Hundreds of hand-drawn swallows were crafted and carefully arranged around a custom script, which together formed a series of meaningful Vietnamese wishes - peace, success and prosperity.

an
Tai
Loc
AN
LÔC
TÀI
an

An

Oye Cariño!

Studio: Futura

Futura designed a typeface that meets up with the fresh color, intriguing mix of fish and vegetables to extend a warm welcome to every customer.

oye CARIÑO!

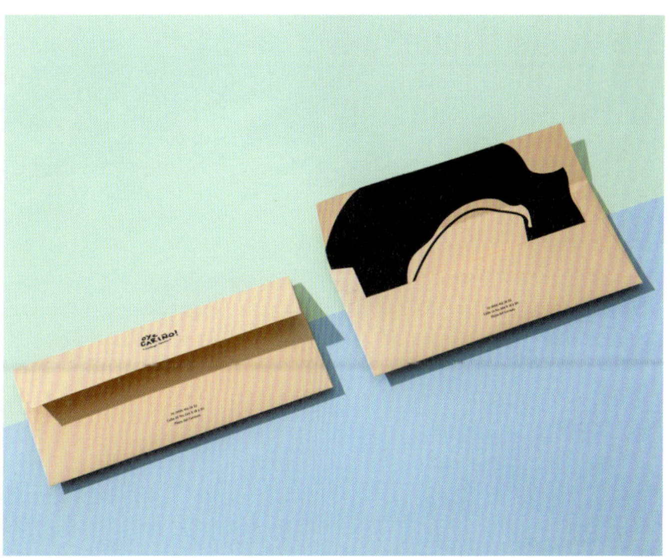

oye CARIÑO!

oye CARIÑO!
PESCADO FRESCO
QUINTANA ROO, MX.
01 (999) 412 38 52
Calle 36 No.344 X 18 y 20
Playa del Carmen
01 (999) 412 38 52
Calle 36 No.344 X 18 y 20
Playa del Carmen

Yellow Bird Tea Series

Designer: Lucy Joy
Copyright: Yellow Bird Project

This project was trying to define the brand with a sense of joy and relaxation, so the designer drew the typeface with an uninhibited and non-mechanical technique, such as using the wobbly lines to express the cozy and warm character of the project.

A FAMOUS BLEND OF CHINESE GREEN TEA

TEA SERIES

ENJOY ERNEST HEMMINGWAY'S FAVORITE DRINK WITH A TWIST!

Subform Identity

Designer: Dennis De Vries
Studio: Subform

Subform is the alias of Dutch graphic designer Dennis de Vries, displaying the logo/typography and placing as a paperclip, referring to the alias - holding sub forms.

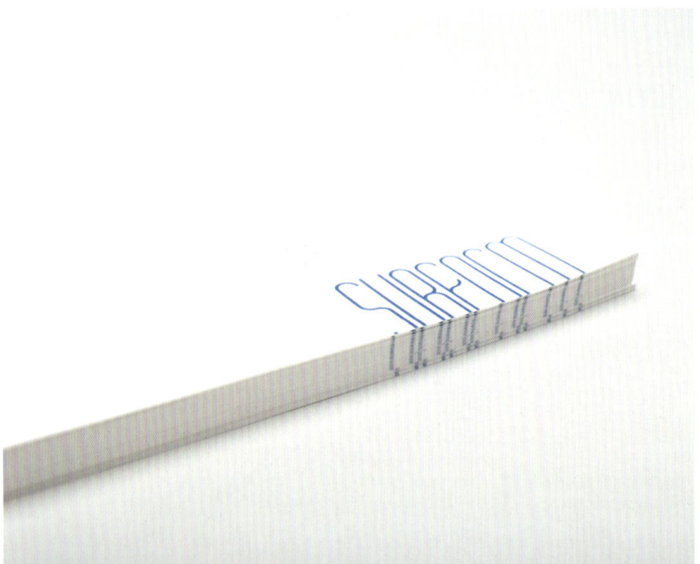

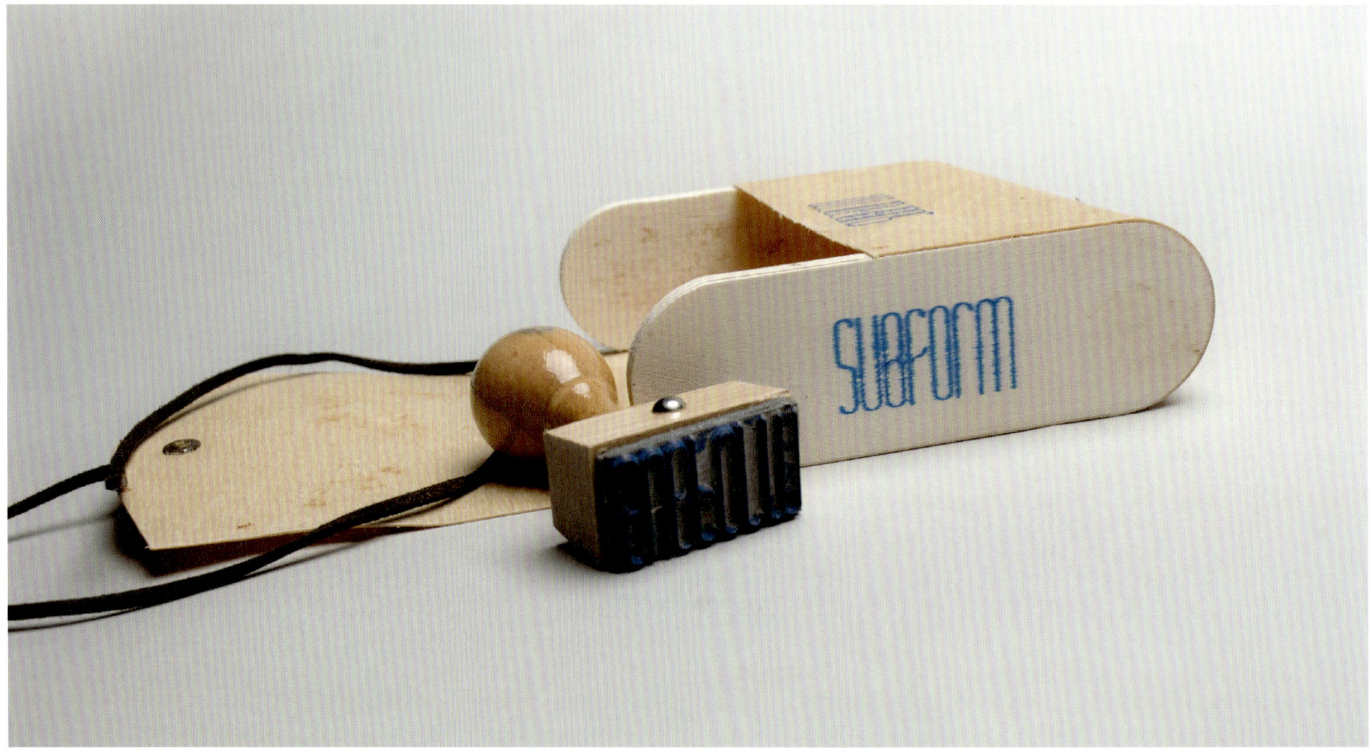

TK Food

Designer: Chien Yun Ho
Studio: Victor Branding Design Corp.

This typeface is designed to meet up with the tourist attraction, conveying a sense of relaxation and playfulness by using cubes which perfectly match the packaging style as well.

Badefun

Designer: Hsin-Yu Chen
Studio: Hsinyu Design

The key visual element of the design is the Chinese characters, meaning badefun. The plentiful Bade culture, urban characters and local snacks are symbolized through the approach of using multiple colors, expressing the concept of "LOHAS is always infinite".

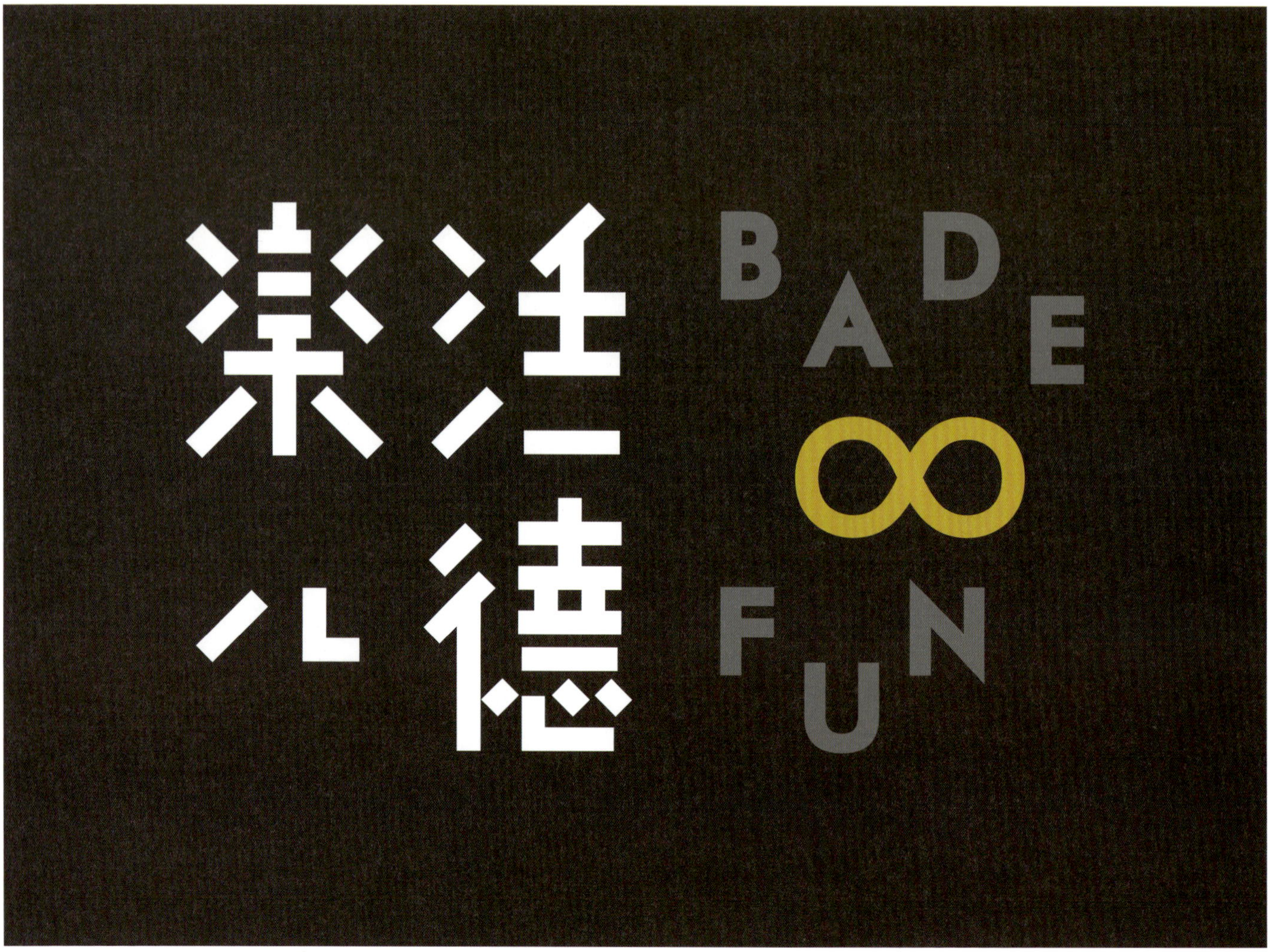

Lucciano's & Burbar

Designer: Panco Sassano

With the aim to provide spaces with their own identity, the designer was seeking to resume historical aspects and aesthetic of the time where this stylish food (hamburgers) popularized, and to give it a contemporary and fresh sensation through typography.

drinks
Just like mom used to make.
Better than the original
1
BIGBUR
SUPERB

tomato

Just like mom used to make.
Burbar

&
A
&CO
Chocolate
a
Finest White Chocolate
№ 1
...Not just GOOD but GREAT.
Vanilla

Masticar 2014

Designer: Yanina Arabena & Guillermo Vizzari
Studio: Yani & Guille

This typeface is hand drawn letters created to express the festive atmosphere of the Argentine gourmet fair and the delightful feeling of food-tasting. The hand made letters correspond to the hand made food by the most prestigious Argentine restaurants and chefs.

COMER
RICO
HACE BIEN
MASTICAR
2014
#MASTICAR
WWW.FERIAMASTICAR.COM.AR
FERIAMASTICAR
ACELGA
HSBC
Buenos Aires Ciudad
BA ESTACIONES SALUDABLES

PÁJARO
QUE
COMIÓ,
VOLÓ

PANZA
LLENA
CORAZÓN
CONTENTO

QUIEN QUIERA
VIVIR SANO
COMA POCO
Y CENE
TEMPRANO

DONDE
COMEN
2
COMEN
TRES

ABREVIAR
LA
CENA,
PROLONGAR
LA VIDA

SOBRE
GUSTOS
NO HAY
NADA
ESCRITO

COMER COMER COMER

RICO RICO

HACE

HACE BIEN BIEN

→ → → →

2014

16, 17, 18, 19 Y Y DE OCTUBRE

El Dorrego EL DORREGO — — /

Distrito Audiovisual W WWW.

FERIAMASTICAR.COM.AR f #

BBGHHJJJKKNNPQQVVXXY

ZZbbccffgghhhhjjjkkmmn

nppqqtvvvwwxxyyzz

¡!¿:;<>?«»&&&©®@@

0 1122334 44556677889 9

()$$ % % ™

ao 023

de

¶ dd

eee 1234567890 1234567890 1234567890 /

New Practices New York 2014

Creative Director: Natasha Jen
Designer: Yenwei Liu
Studio: Pentagram

"New Practices New York" is a biennial competition that serves as New York's preeminent platform to recognize and promote new and innovative architecture and design firms. The 2014 competition was organized around the theme "Action!," and the design for the exhibition extends the strong black lines of the logo into graphics and a custom typeface that run across the walls and floor of the gallery to activate the space.

NEW PRACTICES
NEW YORK

NEW
PRACTICES
NEW
YORK 2014
TAPE FONT

Character Set

ABCDEFGHIJKLM
NOPQRSTUVWXYZ
“”!?[],.

Project Name 10

"THE QUICK BROWN FOX JUMPS OVER THE LAZY DOG."

"WE THINK, RECONSIDER [THINGS] AND RELAX."

"THE CITY INSPIRES AS MUCH AS IT HELPS TO IDENTIFY THINGS TO FIGHT AGAINST."

"WHAT BETTER PLACE TO START A SMALL DESIGN PRACTICE, BUT IN A CITY THAT IS SO EXPENSIVE, HIGHLY REGULATED, AND POLITICAL? PRACTICE HERE MAKES WORKING ELSEWHERE IN THE WORLD FEEL SIMPLE BY COMPARISON."

Project Name 11

Darlings of the Day

Designer: Tom Dabner
Studio: Believe in®

The artwork features a photographic narrative inspired by the title Get Burned. Hand-drawn typography has been created with charcoal for the cover title and back cover track listing.

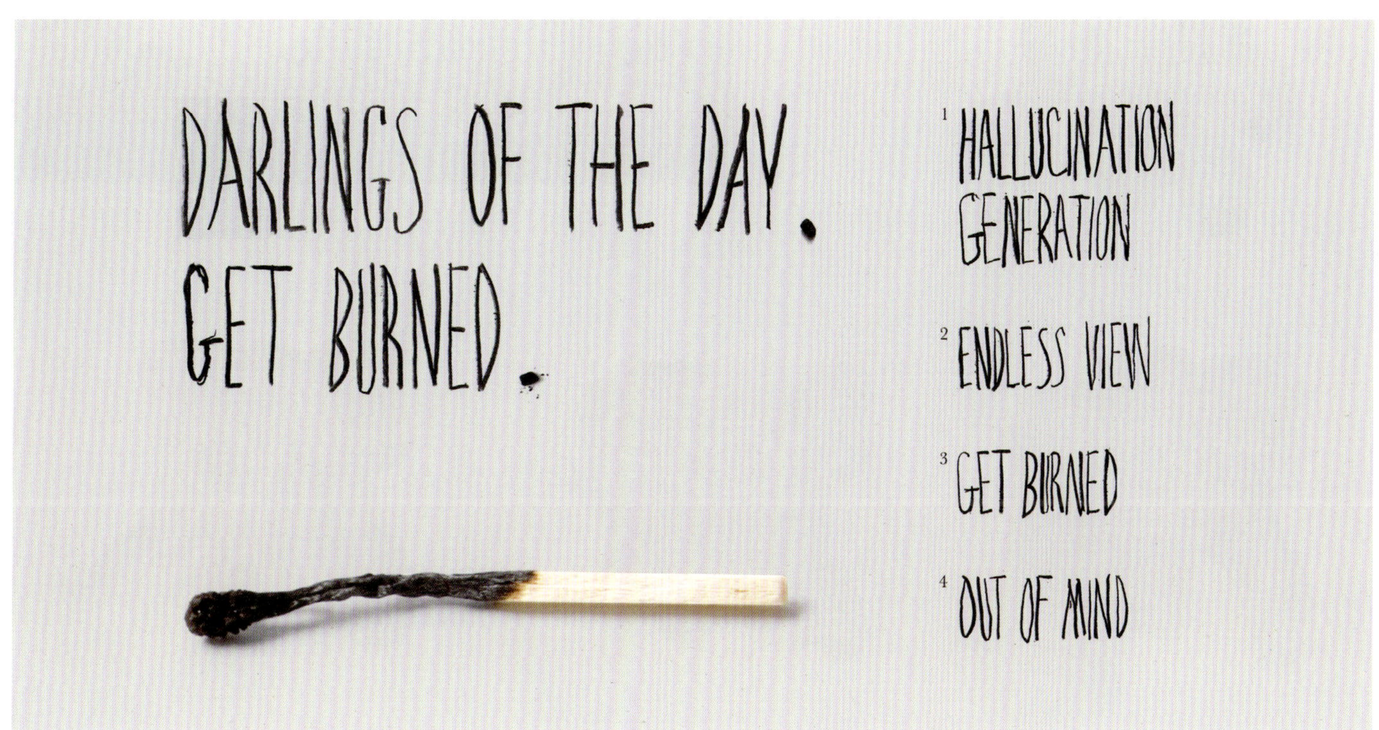

FLOW: The Power of Forward

Organizer: Taiwan Designers' Week

FLOW, the theme of 2012 TWDW, stands for force, link, opportunity and worldwide, symbolizing Taiwanese designers yearning to make TWDW a design joint of Taipei city, a national festival and a global event. The typeface design sought to send out this idea by using fluid lines and stretchable knots.

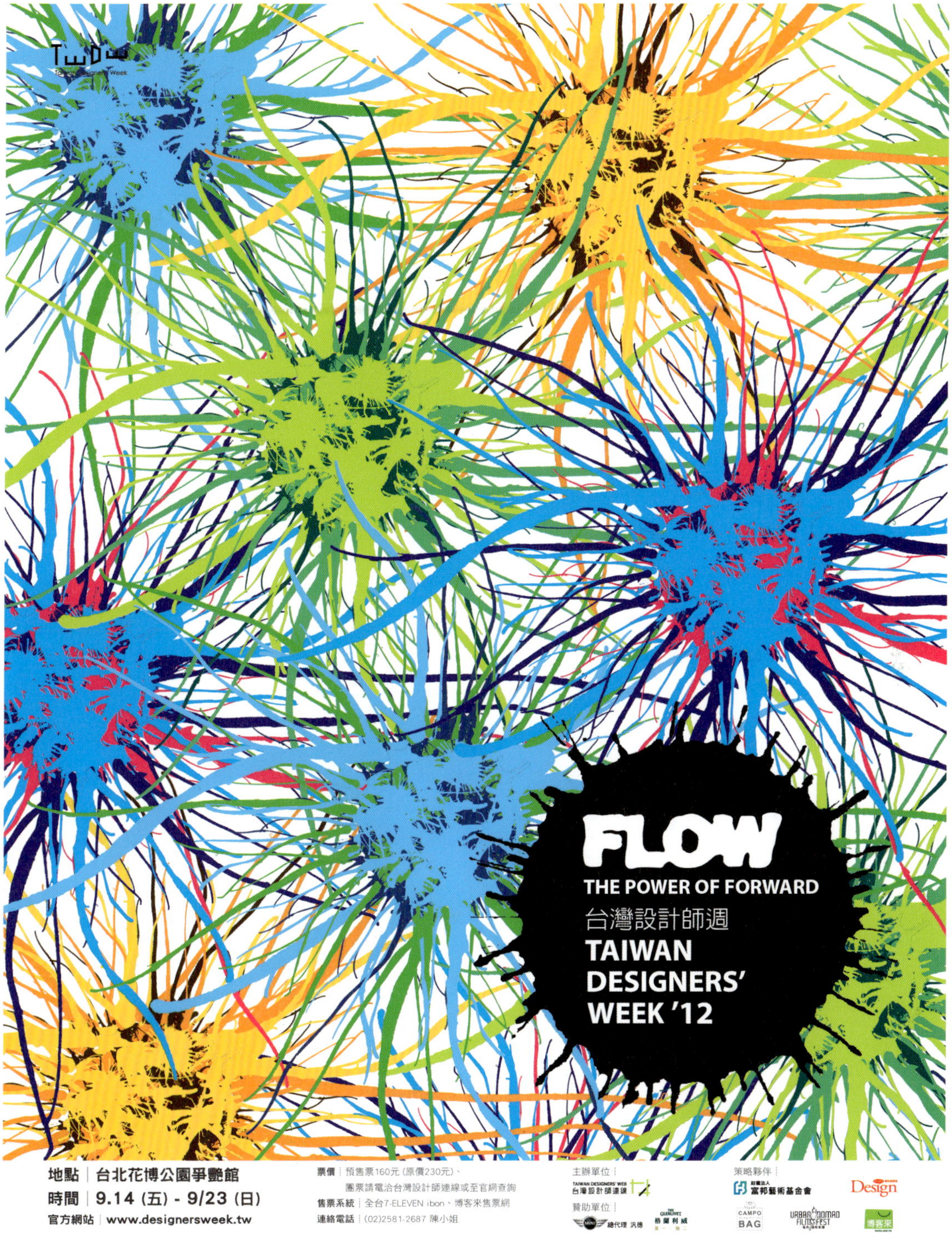

FLOW

THE POWER OF FORWARD

台灣設計師週

TAIWAN DESIGNERS' WEEK '12

地點｜台北花博公園爭艷館
時間｜9.14 (五) - 9/23 (日)
官方網站｜www.designersweek.tw

票價｜預售票160元（原價230元）、團票請電洽台灣設計師連線或至官網查詢
售票系統｜全台7-ELEVEN ibon、博客來售票網
連絡電話｜(02)2581-2687 陳小姐

主辦單位｜TAIWAN DESIGNERS' WEB 台灣設計師連線
贊助單位｜MINI 總代理 汎德　THE GLENLIVET 格蘭利威
策略夥伴｜財團法人 富邦藝術基金會　Design　CAMPO BAG　URBAN NOMAD FILM FEST　博客來

El Cangrejo Films Identity

Designer: Borja Martínez
Studio: Lo Siento Studio

This typeface design conveys the concept of filming and producing by using neon, giving the whole identity a modern sensation while bringing up the memories of old film production.

Porto Explore Interior Design Studio

Designer: Tun Ho

The logo typeface was designed through the irregular orders of writing and regular turnings. In this way, the designer was trying to advocate exploring the possibility of space.

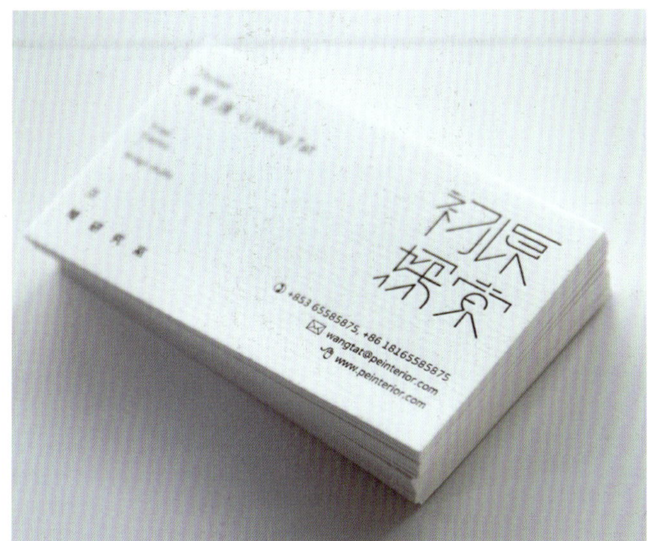

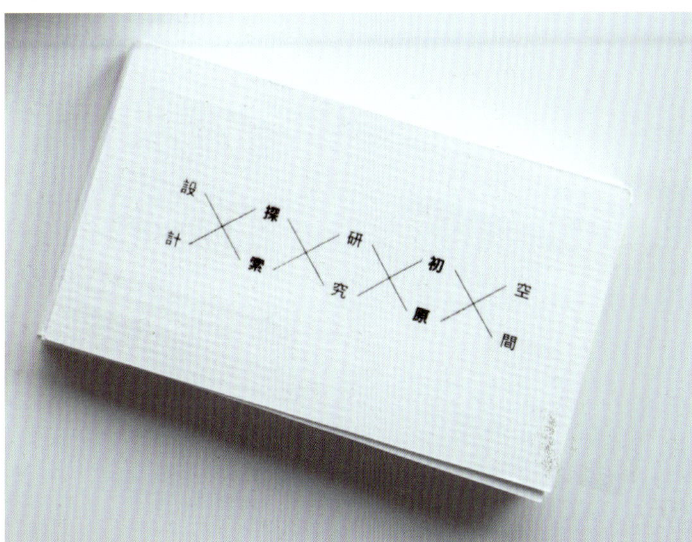

Aizone FW14 / SS15

Creative Director: Stefan Sagmeister/ **Art Director & Designer:** Jessica Walsh
Photographer: Henry Hargreaves/ **Body Painter:** Anastasia Durasova
Creative Retouch: Erik Johansson/ **Hair Stylist:** Gregory Alan
Producer: Ben Nabors & Group Theory/ **Production Designer:** John Furgason & Andy Eklund
Studio: Sagmeister & Walsh

Aizone is a luxury department store in the Middle East. By using scripts painting, this project presented the vibrant nature of the brand in campaigns that were printed in newspapers, magazines, and billboards throughout Lebanon.

FEAR LESS

Tomik

Studio: Province Design Studio

Tomik is a wooden education toy which has been produced since 1999 in Tomsk, Russia. To communicate a sense of playfulness and the features of the toy sets, designers used vivid colors and blocks in the creation process.

Деревянная круглая

АБВГДЕЖЗИКЛМНО
ПРСТУФХЦЧШЩЪЫ
ЬЭЮЯ.,!?

48 деталей
6 карточек
ТОМИК
СЕРИЯ ДЕРЕВЯННЫХ ИГРУШЕК
КОНСТРУКТОРЫ, КУБИКИ, ДОМИНО, ЛОТО, ПИРАМИДКИ, ДОСКИ-ВКЛАДЫШИ
Наборы удачно дополняют друг друга, позволяя ребёнку придумывать увлекательную игру.
ТОМЬ-СЕРВИС
Полный каталог в интернете
www.tomik.ru
+3
Полный каталог в интернете
www.tomik.ru

ТОМИК
ЦВЕТНОЙ ГОРОДОК
14
конструктор тематический
ТОМЬ-СЕРВИС
Полный каталог в интернете
www.tomik.ru
Для детей дошкольного и младшего школьного возраста

ТОМИК
ЦВЕТНОЙ ГОРОДОК
41

ТОМИК
КУБИКИ
ЦВЕТНЫЕ
www.tomik.ru

Insal'Arte

Designer: Mirco Luzzi
Studio: DeOfficina

Designers wanted to create a typeface of hand-crafted feel. Therefore, the inspiration comes from the product itself. The brand is perfectly shaped by the letter forms which articulate the natural and environmentally-friendly character of the brand to customers.

Rucola
INSAL'ARTE
OrtoRomi

INSAL'ARTE
Andace

INSAL'ARTE

Orientali
INSAL'ARTE

INSAL'ARTE

Hum

Designer: Mike Collinge
Studio: DNA

The aim was to create a new brand identity and packaging system for a series of Propolis health products. A bespoke logotype with a strong geometrical rhythm was designed to express the health and well-being aspects of the brand. A subtle New Zealand flavour is suggested through the carved details in the letter forms.

hum™
100% Pure
New Zealand Propolis

2

Artistic Typeface

SPAM Design

Designer: Seth Labenz & Roy Rub
Studio: Topos Graphics

This design strived to learn from the ancient Egyptian pyramids by applying the architectural structure to the design concept, giving a delicate sense of layers and blocks.

1478 Topkapı Sarayı Topkapı Palace
1843 Kuleli Askeri Lisesi Kuleli Military High School
330 Çemberlitaş Constantine Obelisk
1828 Beyazıt Kulesi Beyazıt Tower
1616 Sultan Ahmed Camii Blue Mosque
1900 Botter Apartmanı Botter Apartment
1870 İstanbul Üni. İstanbul Üni.
1891 I. Arkeoloji Müzesi I. Archaeology Museum
1901 Alman Çeşmesi German Fountain
1465 Adalet Kulesi Tower of Justice
1906 St. Antuan Kilisesi St. Anthony of Padua Church
1890 Sirkeci Garı Sirkeci Station
368 Valens Su Kemeri Valens Aqueduct
MÖ 341 BC Kız Kulesi Maidens Tower
1664 Mısır Çarşısı Spice Bazaar
1904 Bosfor Apartmanı Bosfor Apartment
Tarih Mirası
Historical Heritage
Dekoratif Detaylar
İstanbul'un çok uluslu kültürel mirasından esinlenilerek hazırlanan İstanbul Deko yazı karakteri, kentin tarihi yapılarında görülen dekoratif unsurların bir araya getirilmesiyle tasarlanmıştır.
İstanbul Deko is an original typeface inspired by the multicultural heritage of İstanbul and designed with decorative details of the city's historical structures.
Mimari Çeşitlilik
Decorative Details
Architectural Diversity
537 Ayasofya Hagia Sophia
1865 Beylerbeyi Sarayı Beylerbeyi Palace
1548 Şehzade Camii Şehzade Mosque
1871 Çırağan Sarayı Çırağan Palace
528 Galata Kulesi Galata Tower
1909 Büyük Postane Grand Post Office
534 Kariye Müzesi Kariye Museum
1969 Atatürk Kültür Merkezi Atatürk Cultural Center
1800 Hüber Köşkü Hüber House
1831 Narmanlı Han Narmanlı Han
452 Kız Taşı Column of Marcian
1852 Tophane Kasrı Tophane Palace
532 Aya İrini Hagia Irini
1591 Fethiye Camii Fethiye Mosque
413 Kara Surları City Walls
1850 Kamondo Merdivenleri Kamondo Stairs

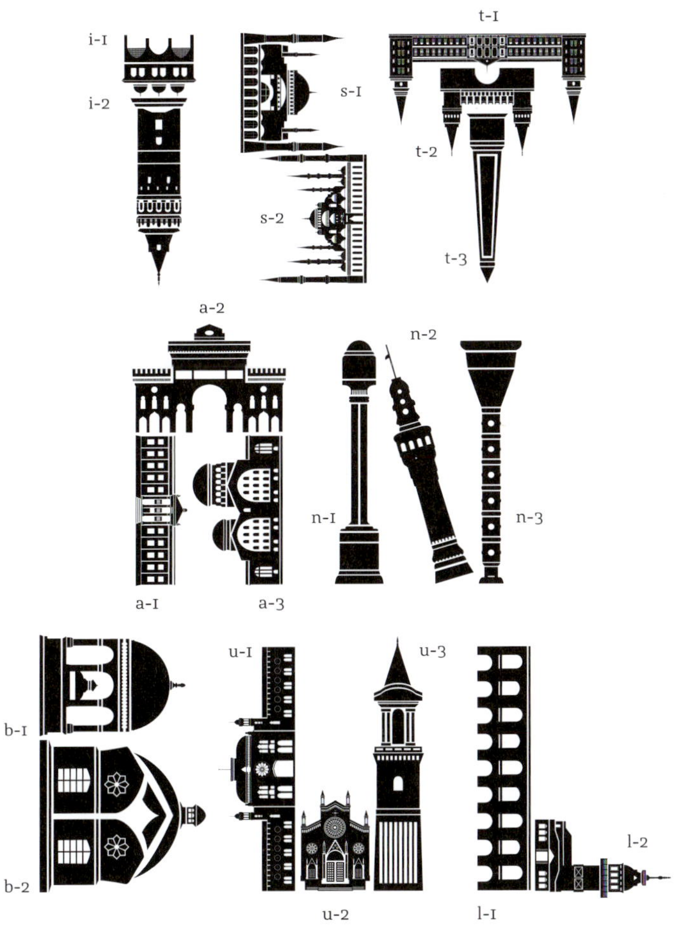

Maiden's Tower
341 BC

St. Anthony of Padua Church
1906

Blue Mosque
1616

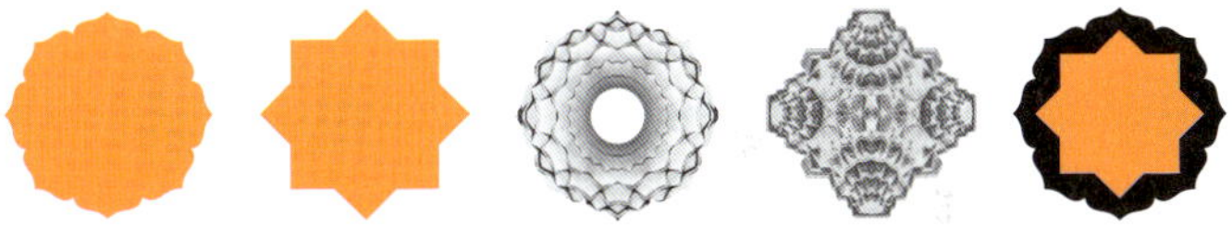

Istanbul Deko Type

Designer: Geray Gencer

Istanbul Deko Type project is designed by using common theoretical base of architecture and typography. Various decorative details from Istanbul's historical structures have been combined in letter forms in order to present the multicultural heritage of Istanbul and the architectural diversity of its history.

TEDxTaipei2014

Designer: Chu-Chieh Lee
Studio:Bito Studio

The English typeface of "WHAT MATTERS NOW" assembles itself into the Chinese characters in negative space. The combination of the eastern and western typefaces also symbolizes the massive changes and influences that TED has experienced in the Chinese society.

*

EMPO typeface

Estudio: LOSIENTO
Diseño: Gerard Miró

* Alfabeto realizado por formulación matemática basado en la fórmula de pitágoras:

Distancia real = Raiz cuadrada de la suma de los cuadrados de la diferencia entre coordenadas correspondientes

Empo

Designer: Borja Martínez & Gerard Miró
Studio: Lo Siento Studio

Designers got inspired by the volumetric forms of organs and bone structure. Through Pythagoras' theorem, they developed each letter form in horizontal level and used beige cardboard to better imitate the bone color.

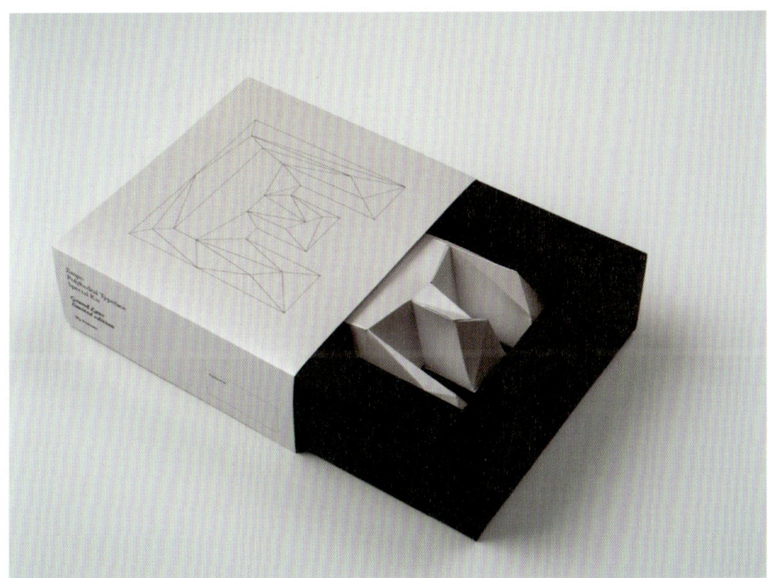

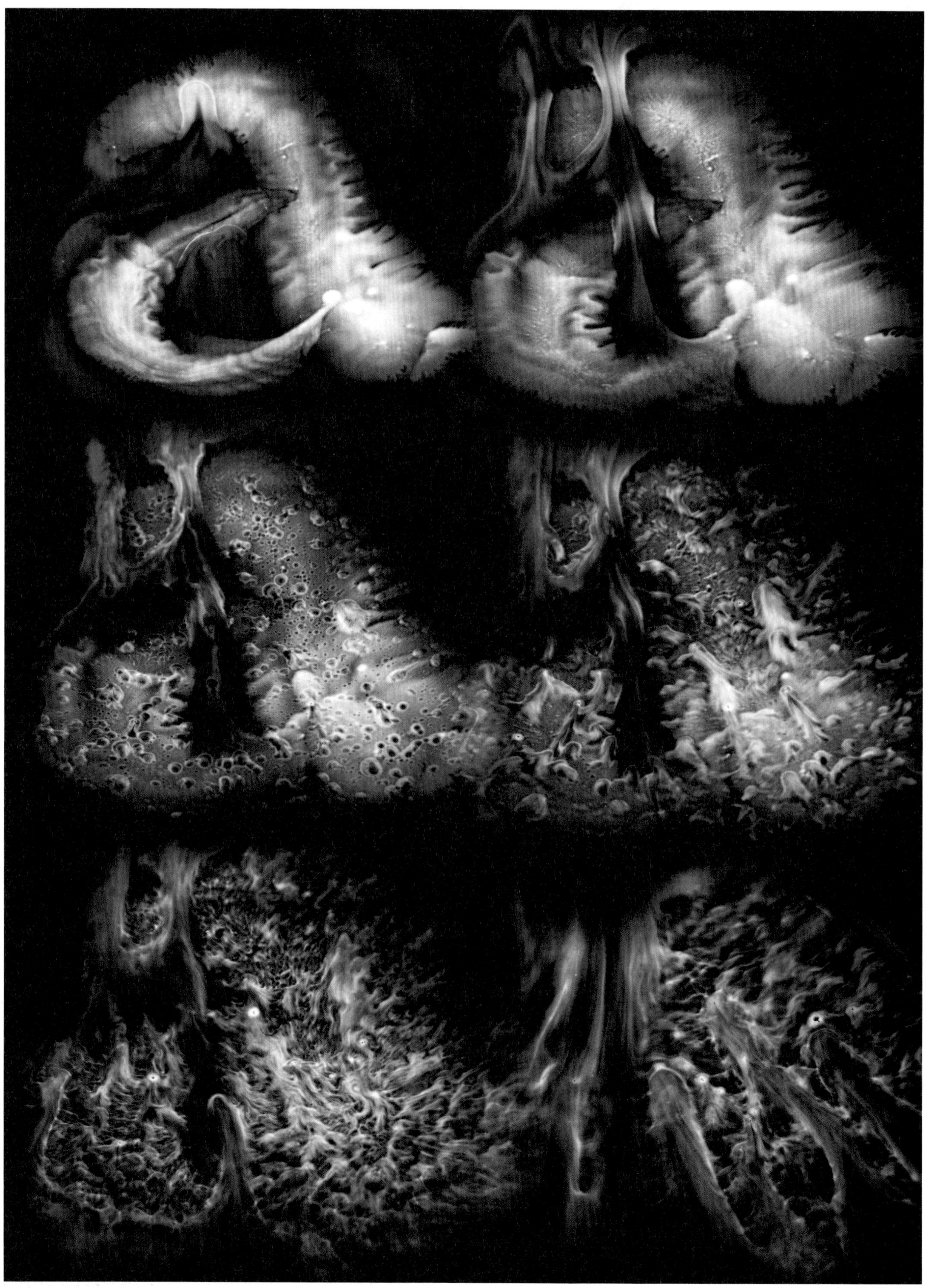

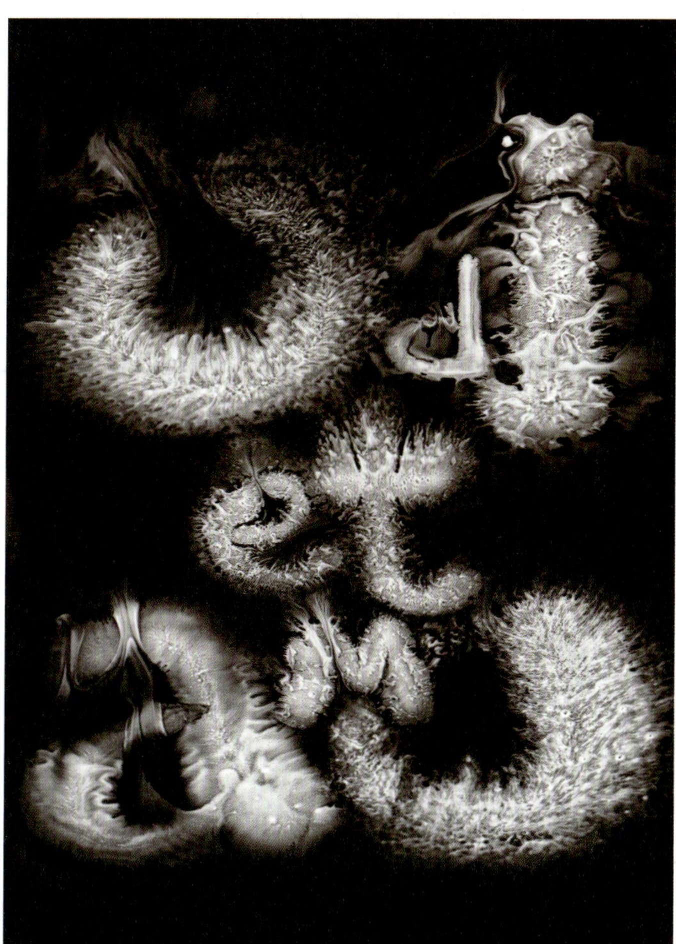

Liquid Type

Designer: Ruslan Khasanov

The project was inspired by using ink on paper to achieve a spreading effect. Ruslan drew the letter on a wet sink surface. The letter came to life: black fine lines instantly flowed, overgrew with gray patterns like coral and then disappeared.

Fashion Font

Designer: Yvette Yang

Fashion Font was created according to the concept "Image is message". The designer used collage method and tried to explore the maximum possibilities of body parts matching.

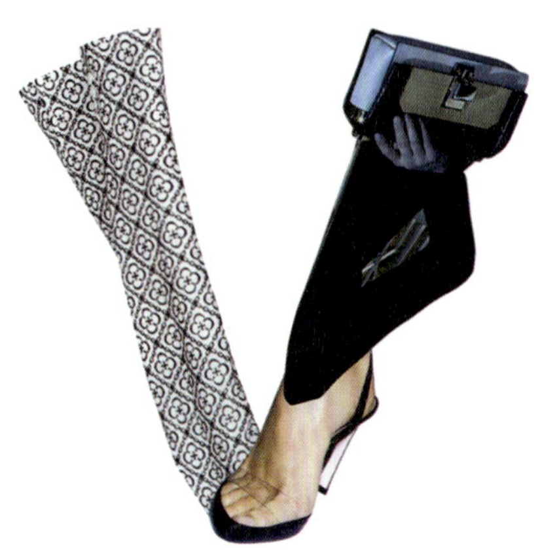

Cardboard Alphabet

Designer: Antonio Rodrigues Jr

By utilizing six basic shapes, the handmade modular system is set up to form different unique letters in an elegant and flexible manner.

Dekoratio Branding & Design Studio Identity and Interior Design

Designer: kissmiklos
Photographer: Bálint Jaksa

Designed types of the studio's motto, strategy and goals appear around interior spaces, giving visitors a comic and creative feel of the company's values and personality.

by Paul
CASH

WOW!
DEKORATIO

DEKORATIO FUN

lOREM
IPSUM

HALADÓ
KONZERVATÍV
LAZA-JÓFEJ
ERŐLTETETT
BARÁTSÁGOS
HIVATALOSKODÓ
IDIÓTA
BEVÁLLALÓS
KONVENCIONÁLIS
KÖZÉPSZERŰ
ÁTLAGOS
STÍLUS

CÉL
N°1
Branding & Design Stúdió
legyünk Magyarországon.
Aztán Európában.

STRA-
TEGIA
SZUPERCSAPAT
A legjobbat tudjuk nyújtani
TANULÁS
HUB
NEMZETKÖZI TAPASZTALATOK
ÜGYFÉLÉLMÉNY
Inspiráló élmény legyen velünk dolgozni
STÚDIÓ
SHOWROOM
PROFI FOLYAMATOK
IMIDZS
Látszon, hogy faszák vagyunk
GIGAWEB
PORTFÓLIÓ
WORN WITH PRIDE
ISMERTSÉG
Minél többen találkozzanak a nevünkkel
BLOG
EVENTS
ONLINE MARKETING

01. ÉRTÉKEK
Design mindenek felett
Csak profin
02. 03.
Igényesen vagy sehogy
Legyünk jobbak
04.

Life in the Alphabet

Designer: Eibatova Karina

By mirroring the natural and mythical creatures' various postures, the designer extracted the essential components of the letter forms and combined them with a sense of mystery. Out comes a set of wonderful alphabet.

Botanical Caps Poster

Designer & Illustrator: Sasha Prood

Through exquisite observation of flowers and plants, the designer created a set of typography resembling the forms and shapes of the elegance and calmness of those natural beauties.

3D Typology

Designer: Dan Hoopert

These typography projects explore the possibilities of producing typeface in 3D effect. The lines were drawn and cropped into the letterforms using Adobe Illustrator and then converted to splines and extruded in Cinema 4D.

ABCD
EFGHI
JKLMN
OPQR
STUV
WXYZ

Aa
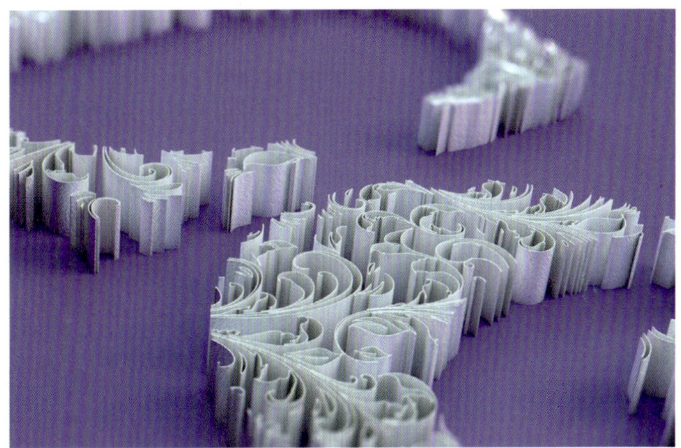

Think
eight
hours
work
two
hours
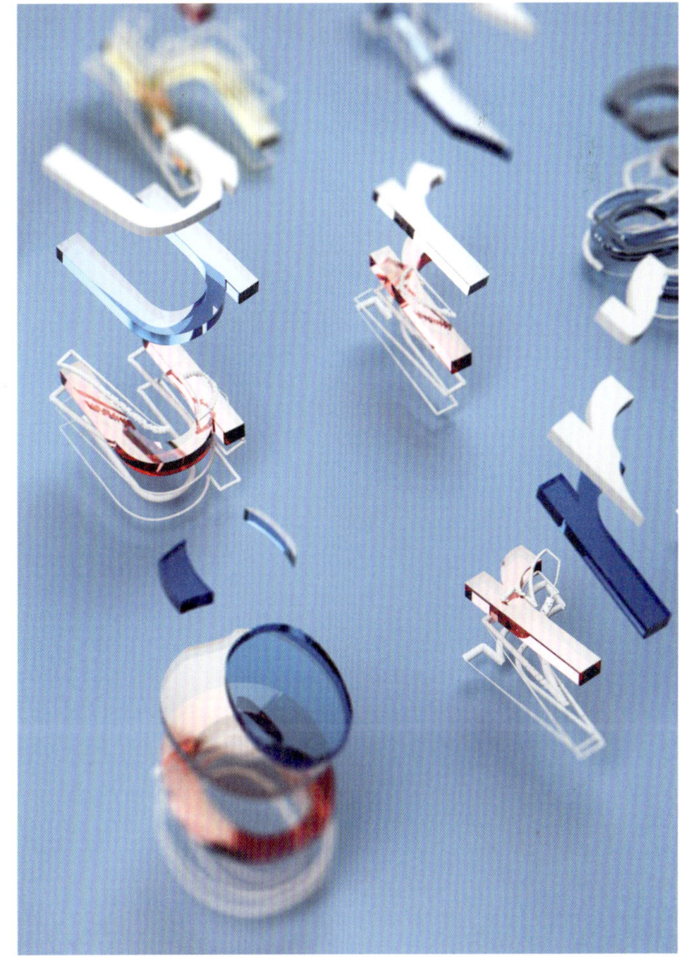

Typography Set

Designer: Ruslan Khasanov

The designer strived to create letters with different materials and tools in an experimental way, presenting typeface in unimaginable angles, such as a microscope.

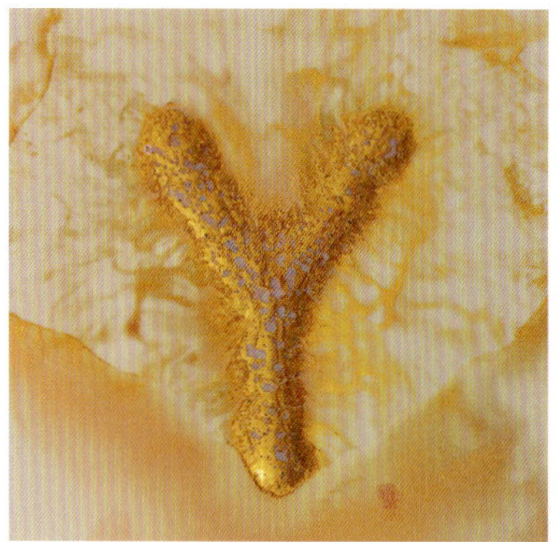

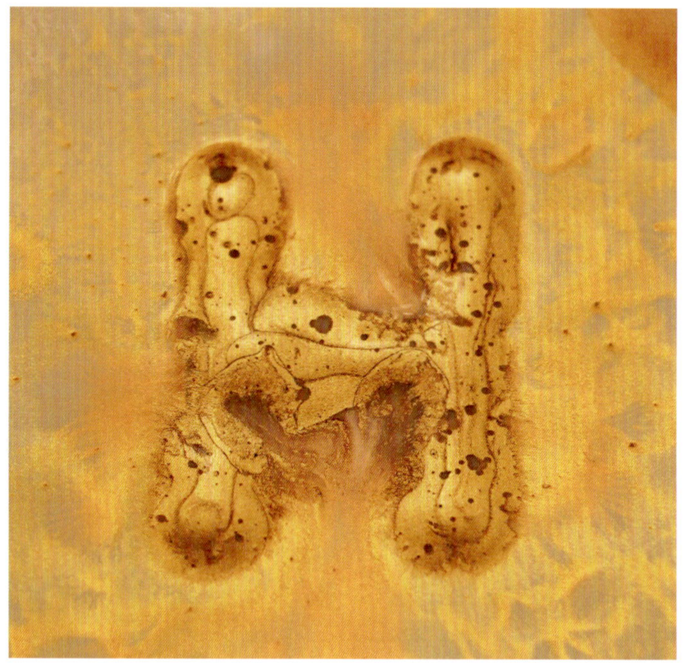

Coral Type

Designer: Dan Hoopert

This typeface is designed to resemble the corals which have many different poses and forms. With the use of wires in triangle shapes, letters were formed in a solid and natural style.

Creative Alphabet

Designer: Xavier Casalta

This is a collection of letters illustrated in different styles and inked with a stippling technique. Through this project, the designer wanted to create an entire alphabet in which each letter will have its own personality.

Yorokobu

Designer: Joluvian

The designer deliberately chose to create this letter form with chalks. The use of chalks perfectly demonstrated the line with a sense of dust quality and fluidity.

Simple Things

Illustrator: Sasha Prood

These hand-painted letters were developed as a fresh, light and organic graphic. Mixed with water, leaves and petals, this serene typography is an appropriate way to welcome warmer months.

The Cannonball

Studio: Lo Siento Studio

The designer had the inspiration from Dave Sedgwick and created letter forms using an unexpected material - those little cannonballs.

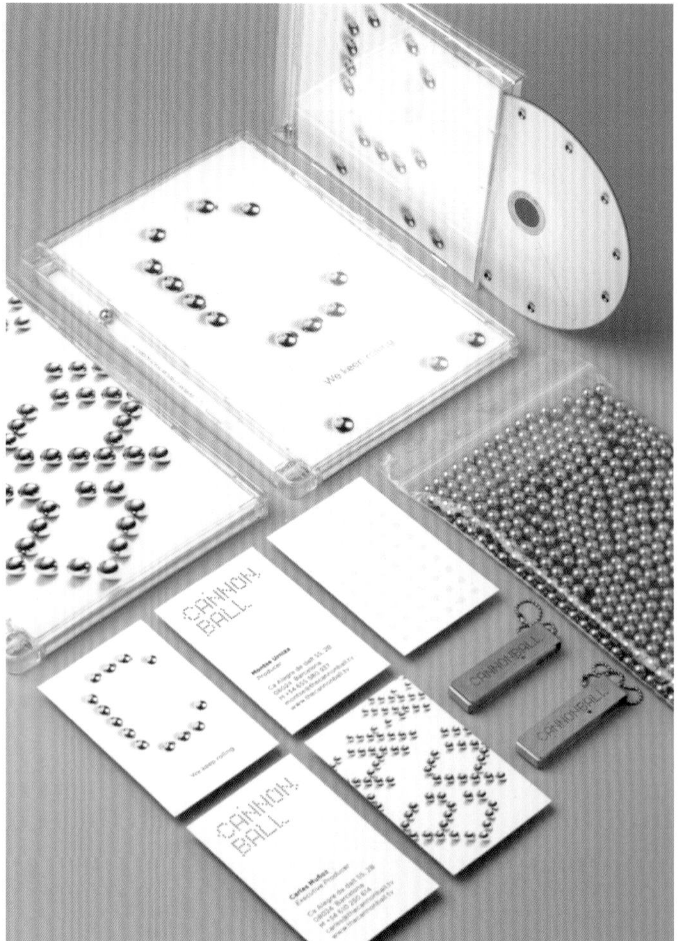

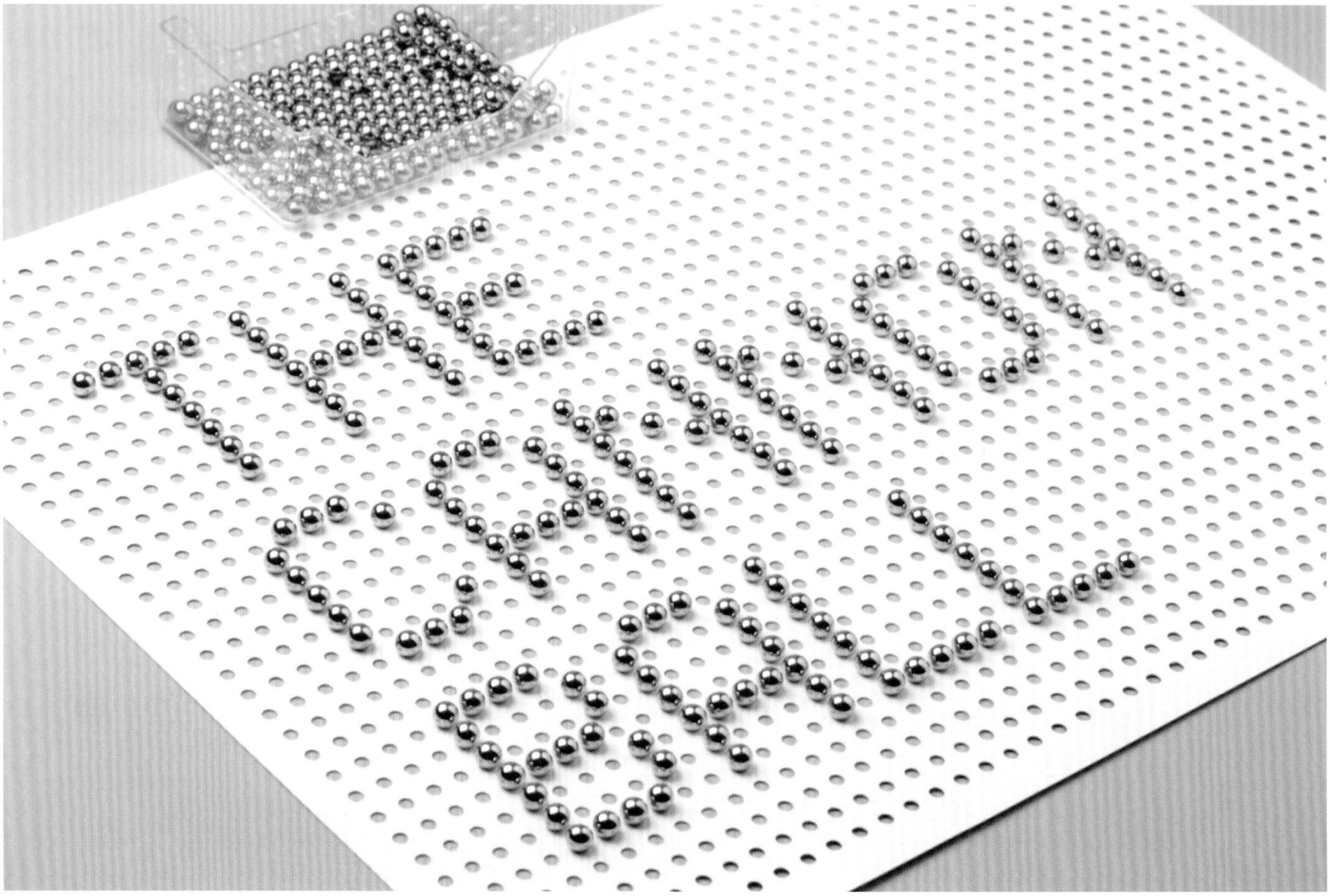

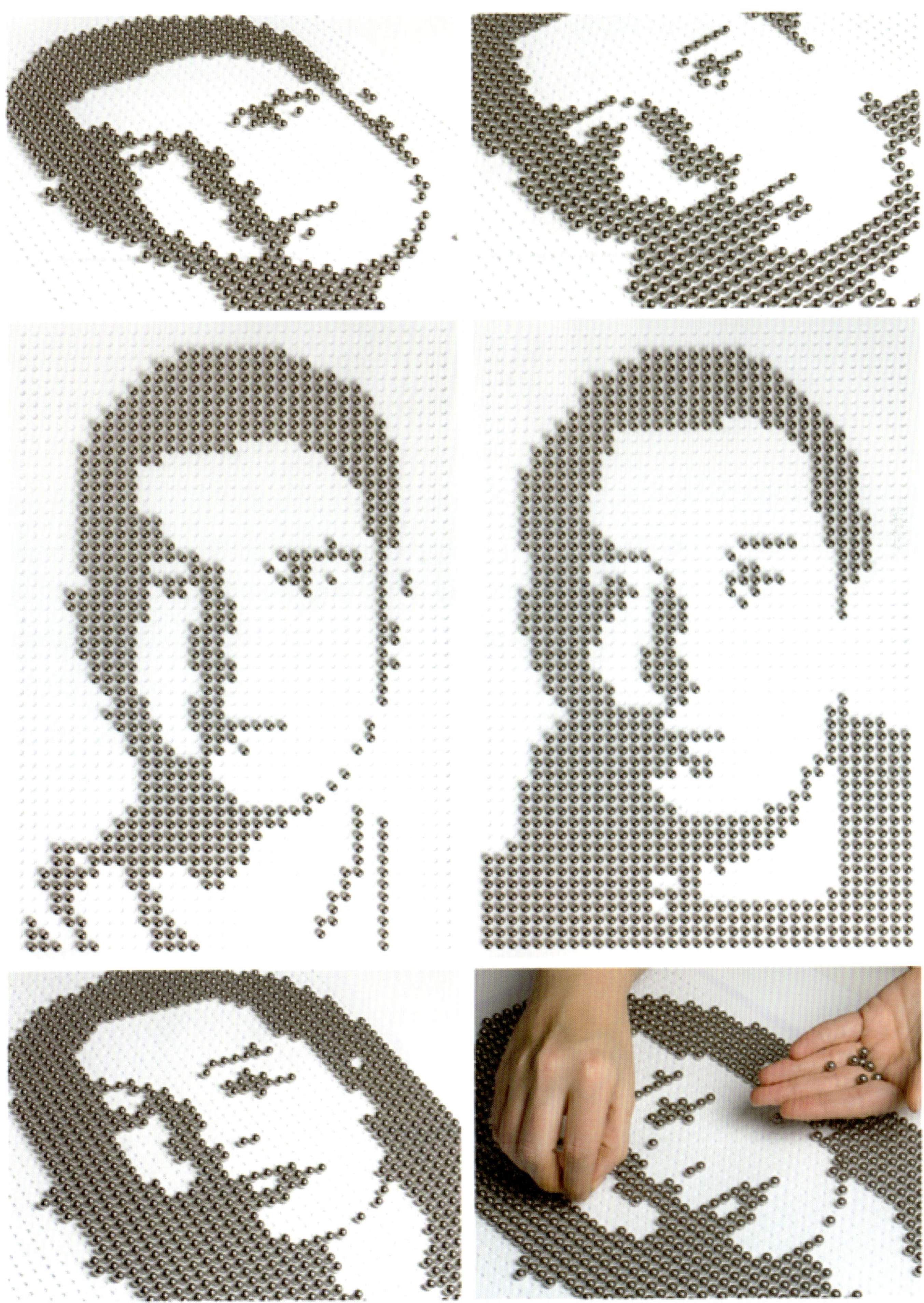

Make Our Pins Green

Designer: Carolina Beiertz

The designer used organic materials such as flower buds, leaves and stems to create this visual piece. The design instils the concept of closeness with nature, and was used in support of a Greenpeace campaign against the use of fossil fuels and to inspire a greener internet.

Bologna Children's Book Fair 2012

Designer: Riccardo Sabatini

The eureka moment came when the designer thought of the randomness of children kneading and tearing paper without reasons. To agree with the book fair's theme, he creatively demonstrated this randomness by creating typeface of twisted, kneaded and folded paper.

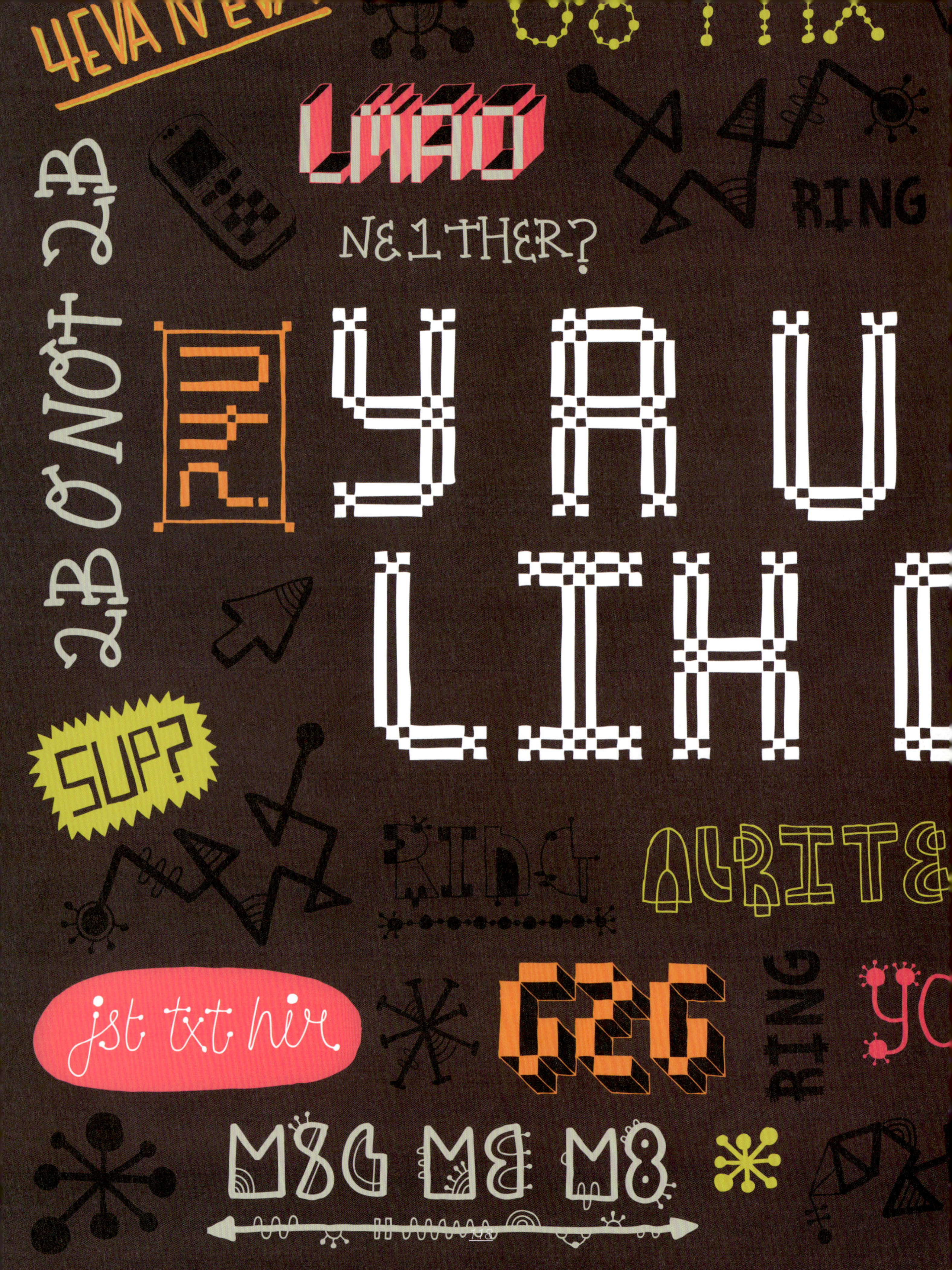

LMAO
RING
NE1THER?
2B OR NOT 2B
Y R U
SUP?
RING
ALRITE
jst txt hir
G2G
RING
MSG ME M8

Y R U SPKN LIK DIS 4

Designer: Gareth Leyshon

Inspired by the changing media, this typeface combines various digital factors with popular quotes, making it fun and joyful.

3

Rhythm of Typeface

Chinese Tea Identity

Designer: Pang Guoping

The development of Chinese tea involves not only the improvement of production process but also the spiritual core of Confucianism, Iaoism and Buddhism. To endow the brand "不可不茶" with historical connotations, the designer strived to extract the essence from Chinese traditional poetic images of cloud, stone, running water and bamboo.

TM

WEI-WU-YIN 2016 Program Guide

Studio: Onion Design Associates

Surrounded by the green field, Wei-Wu-Ying (The National Kaohsiung Center for the Arts) .The shape of 3 hanzi, Wei-Wu-Ying, is inspired by the outline of the building structure. The curve lines response to the continuous outlines of the eaves.

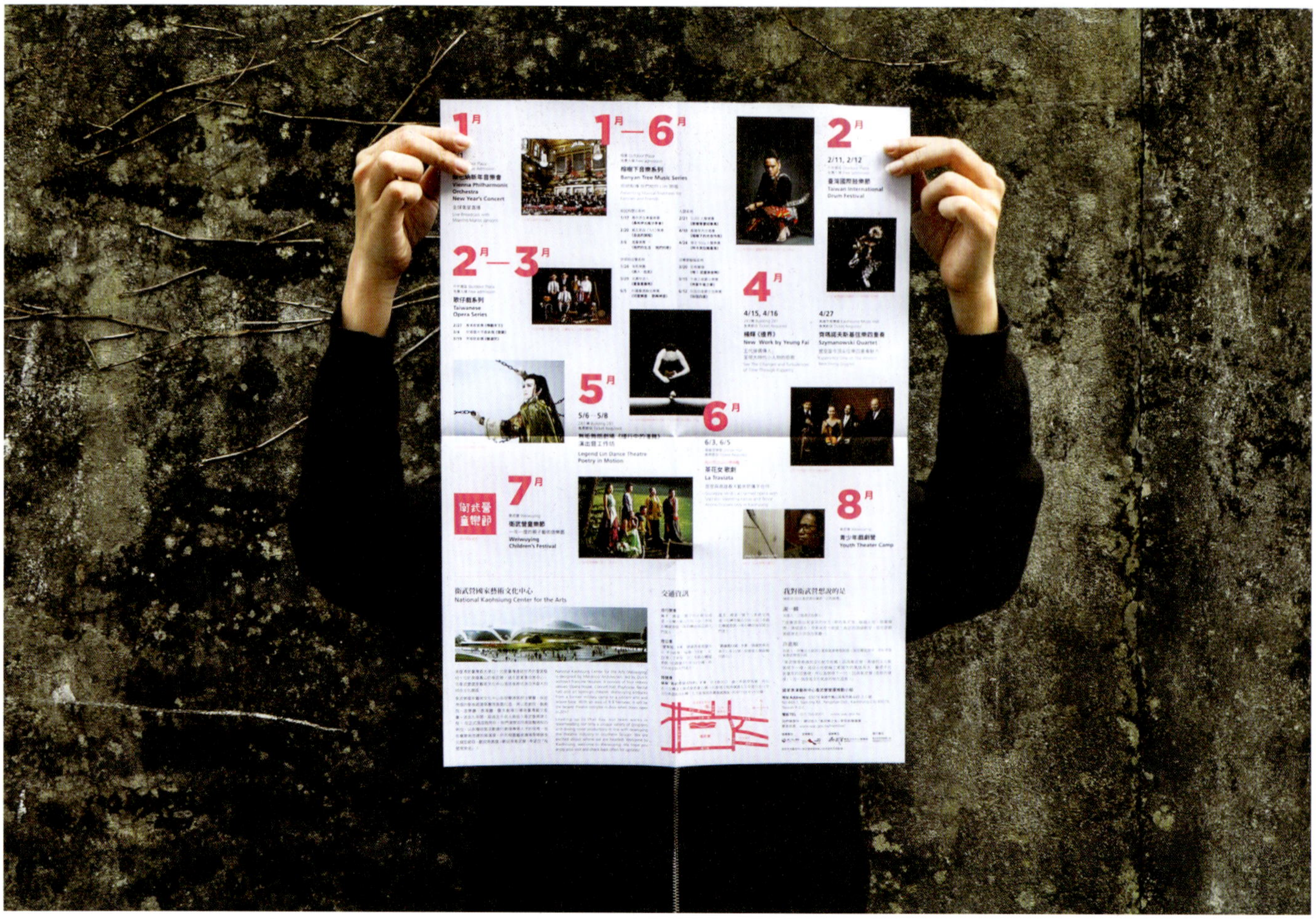

WEI
WU
YING
2016
衛武營
WEI-WU-YING
2016 JAN — AUG
節目指引
01—08

Second Hand Orchestra

Designer: Mattias Amnäs
Studio: Bedow

This is the visual identity and packaging for Second Hand Orchestra's eponymous album and was released on the Sing a Song Fighter label. The tracks on the album were originally recorded for a documentary series, but when the project was cancelled the band leader Karl-Jonas Winqvist decided to reuse the music for an LP — now under the name Second Hand Orchestra.

SECOND HAND ORCHESTRA

Mr. Hormone by TOLAKU

Studio: Onion Design Associates

The new album "Mr. hormone" dealing with the theme of lust and the desire of love. The band members drowning in the sea of endless white liquid symbolize the overflowed of desire and loneliness confronting mid-age crisis of band members. The members resting naked on the liquid is also a metaphor for the band's rebirth.

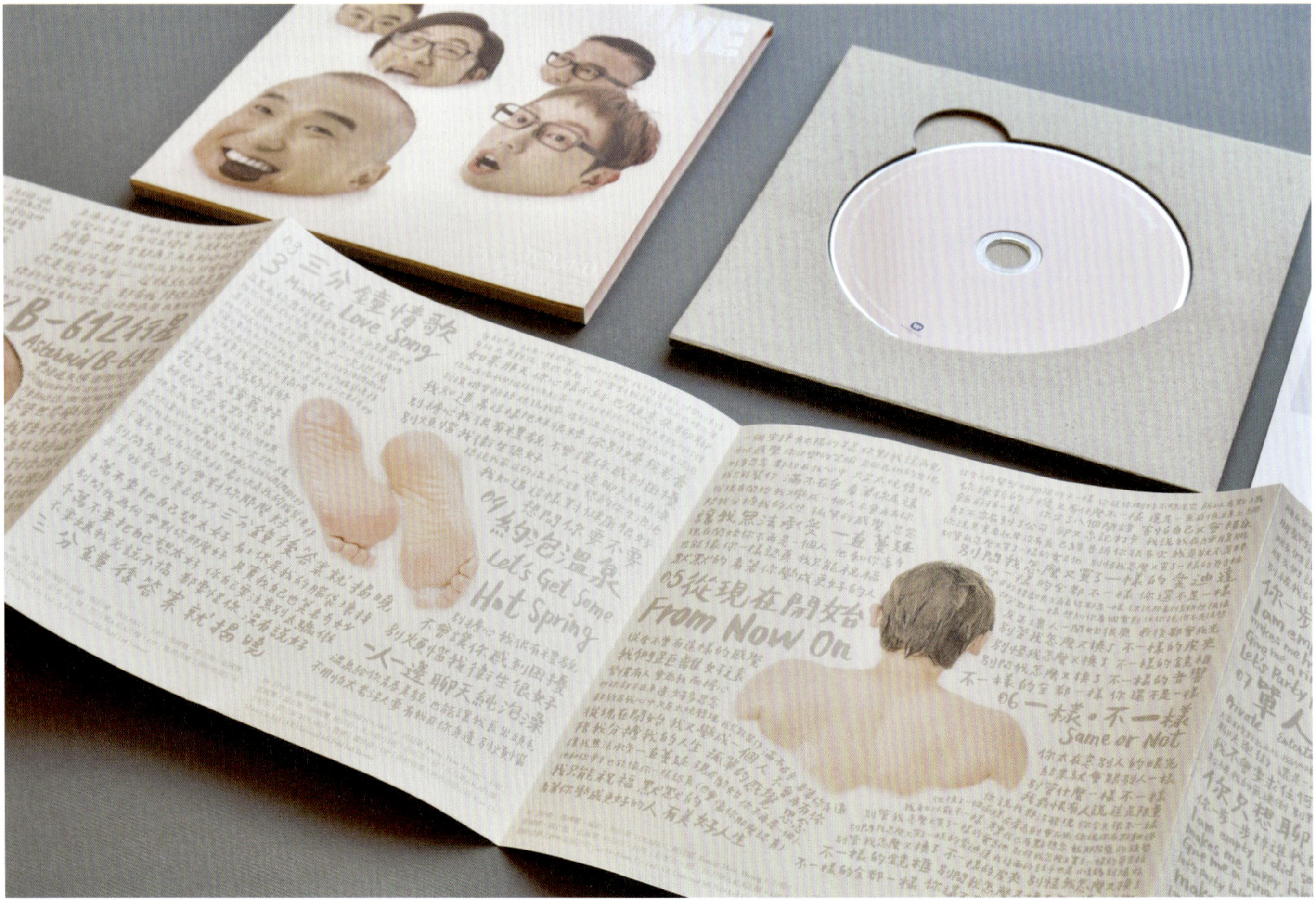

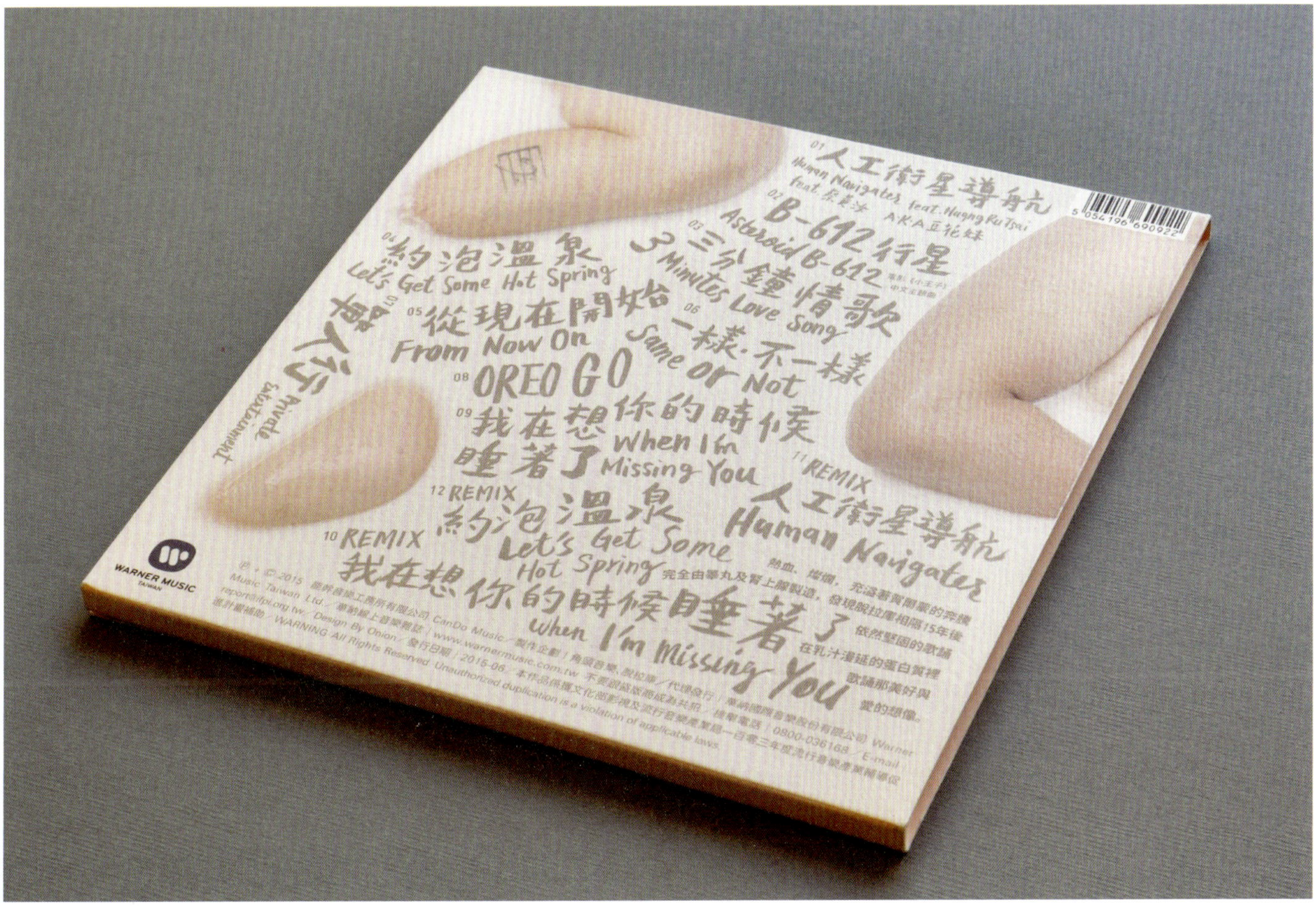

GEOM Display Typeface

Designer: Danilo Gusmão Silveira
Studio: HAW Design Studio

GEOM is a free display type inspired by basic geometric forms and grids. By adept application of lines and squares, this typeface design shows not only its rigidity but also its adaptability to colors and content.

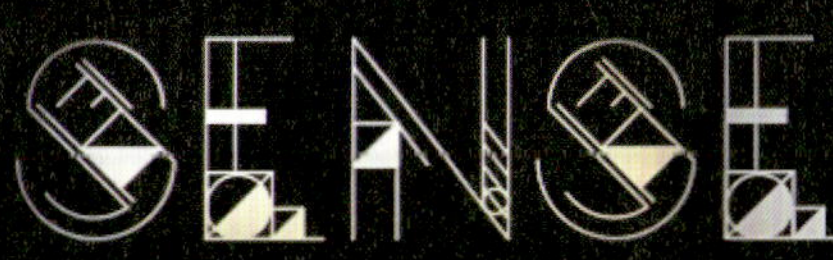
SENSE
dogmusic
Vol 2

005. Lorem Ipsum is simply
dummy text of the printing
and typesetting industry.

Penny Sparkle - Blond Redhead

Studio: Triboro Design

This type design is aimed to redefine the constantly evolving band as a band that can maintain its particular characteristics when exploring the possibility of alternative rock. To achieve that, the designer displayed a liberal typeface featured with wave and fluid.

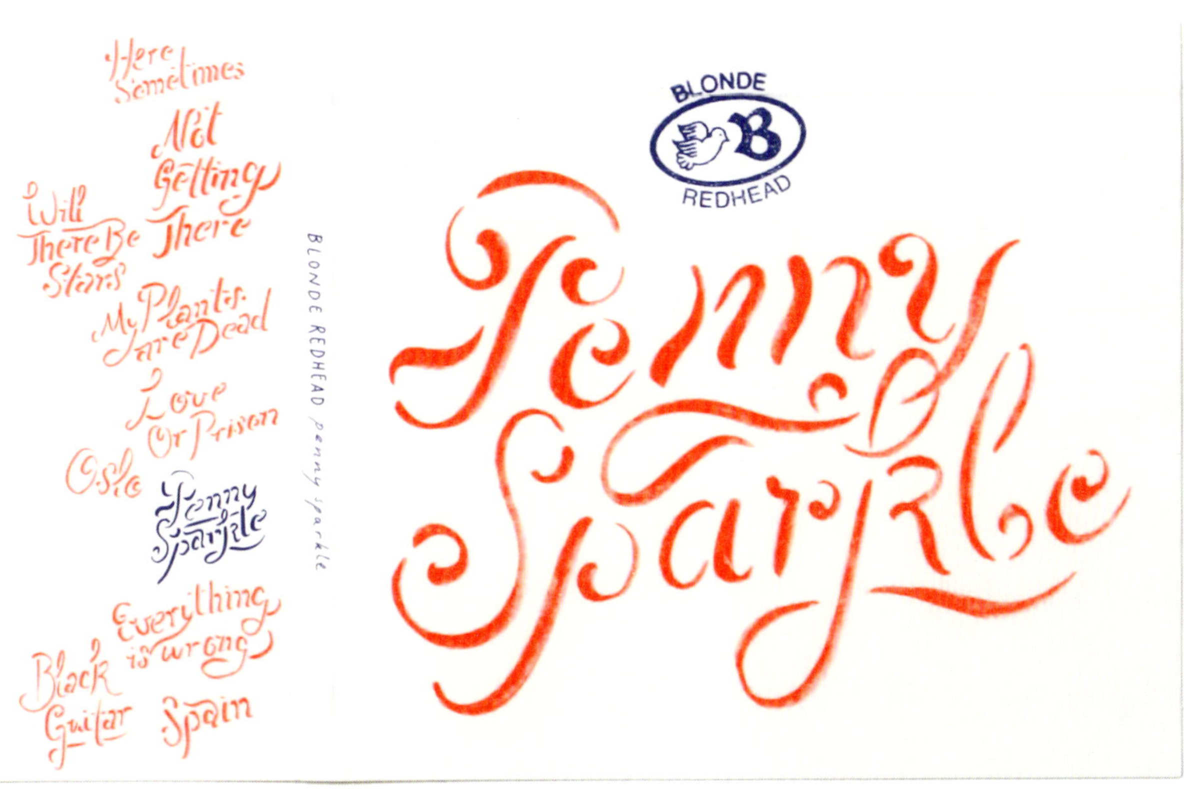

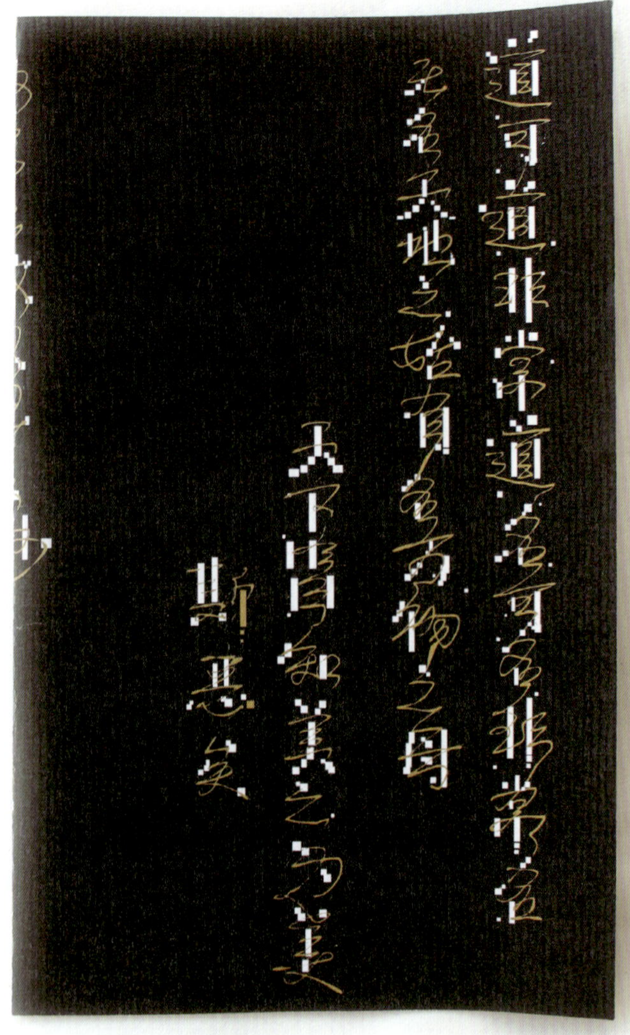

Orientalism

Designer: Grant Ru-Li
Studio: L3

It is a typography inspired by the "Tai Chi and Bagua map". The designer referred to the rhythm and feature of Chinese calligraphy, and abstracted the structure of calligraphy in two directions: horizontal strokes are presented by spiral lines, while vertical strokes pixels.

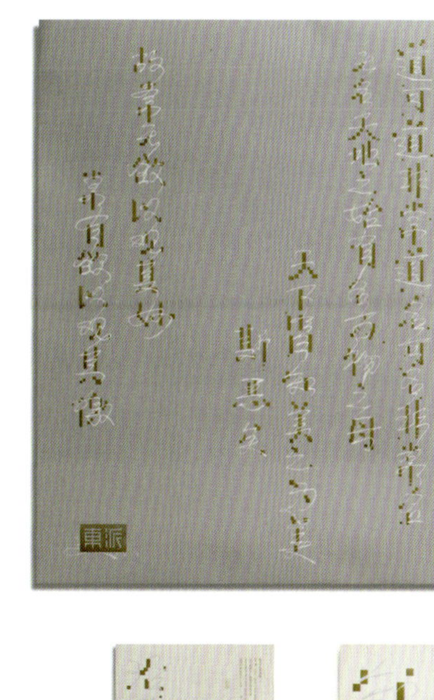

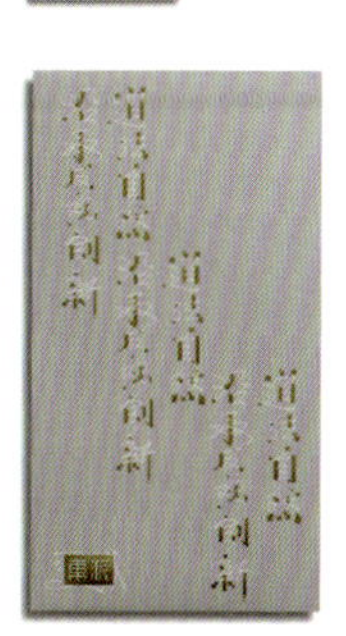

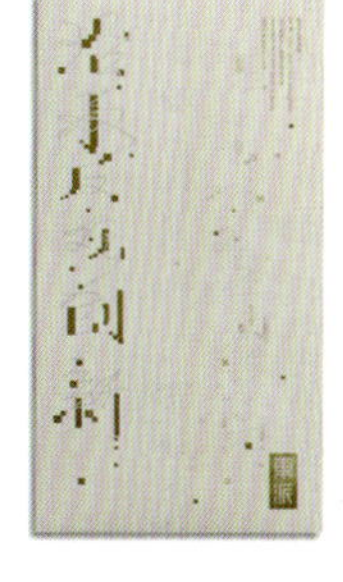

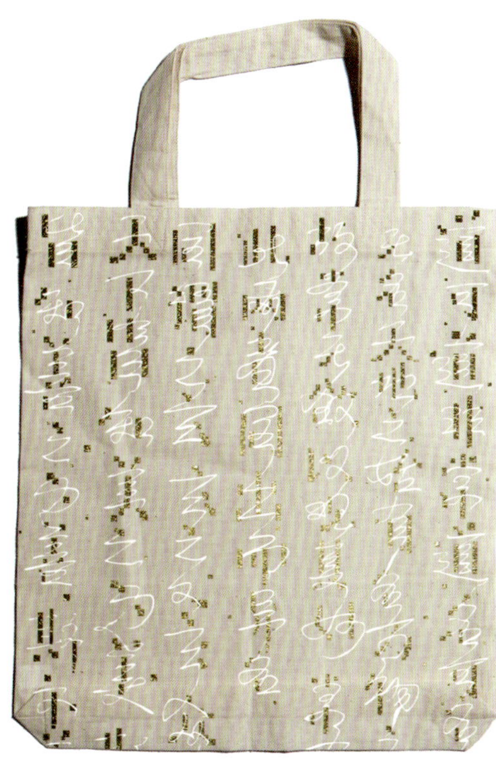

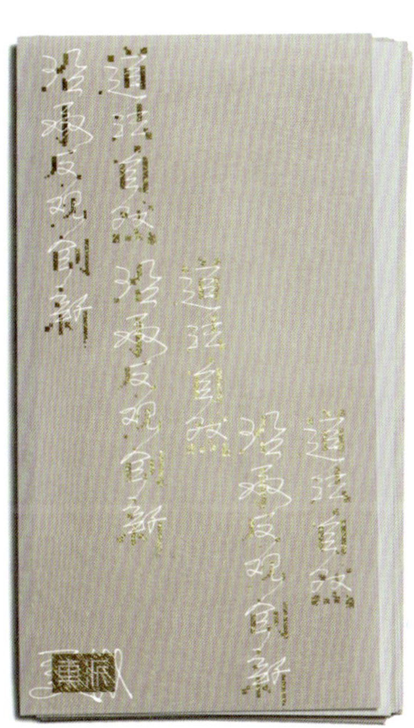

CS Zero

Designer: BenChalit Sagiamsak

In order to be creative and interesting, this project was designed with old school and modern elements. CS Zero contains two different styles and has over 60 letter designs. It has been designed to create diversity to the work pieces.

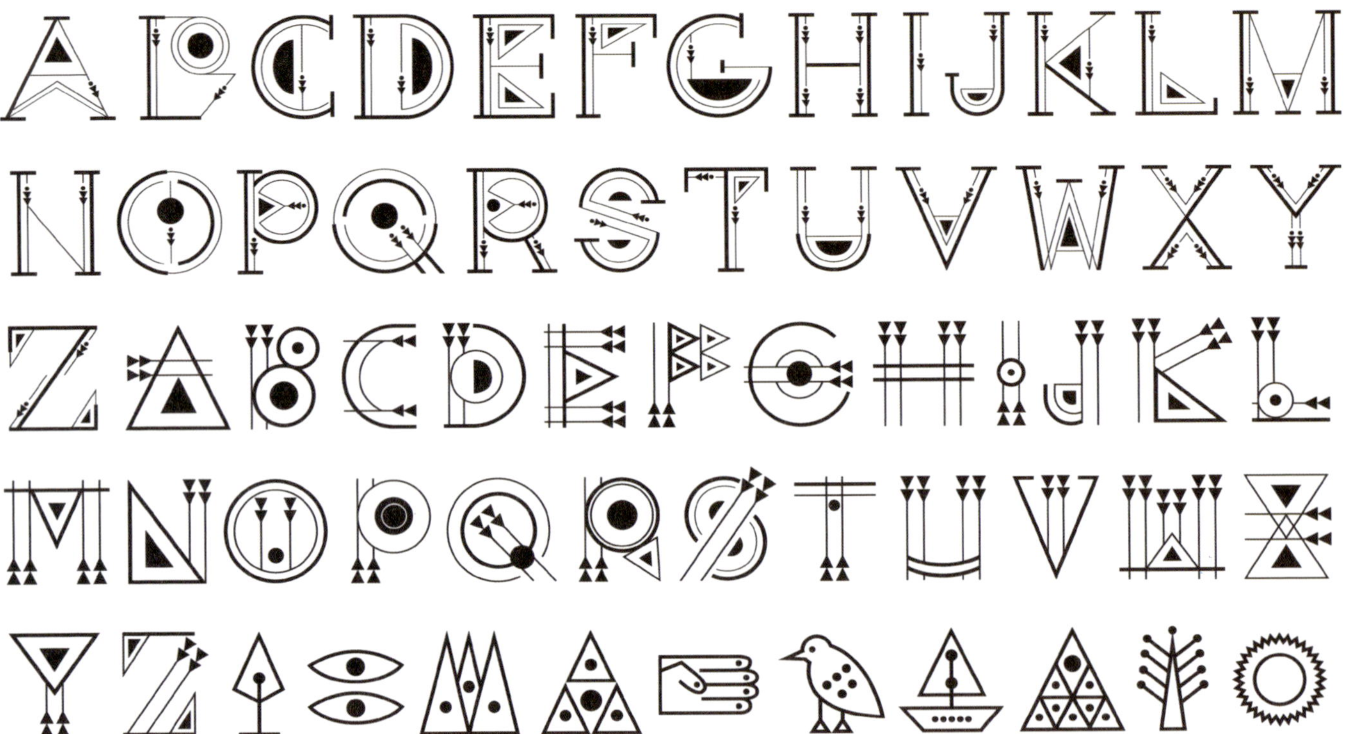

TYPE

HOW TO USE

MODULAR APPLICATION

MODULAR APPLICATION

Fogtype

Designer: Jimbo Bernaus
Studio: Dual Brain Studio

Fogtype is a modular typography born with the intention of breaking schemes. The alphabet and illustrations are based on the repetition of basic and smart forms.

fog

abc
defg
hijklm
nopqrs
tuvw
xyz
FOGTYPE

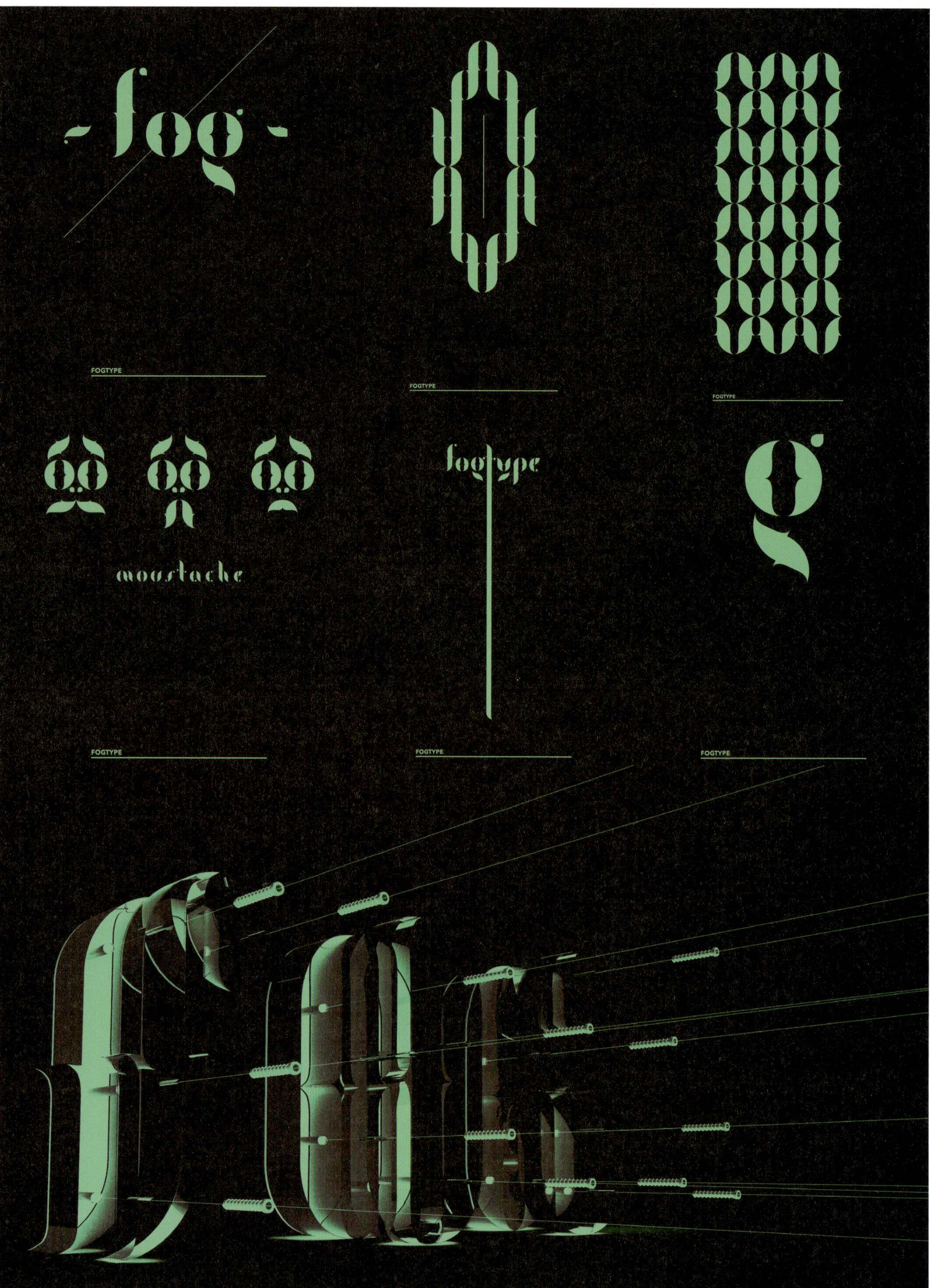

fog
FOGTYPE
FOGTYPE
FOGTYPE
moustache
fogtype
FOGTYPE
FOGTYPE
FOGTYPE

abc

defg

hijklm

nopqrs

tuvw

xyz

FOGTYPE

Foresee Typeface

Designer: Arnaud LE ROUX
Studio: Genosia

The designer focused on the shapes of the type and tried to work on straight lines with various rotations and doubled lines, offering more interesting variations.

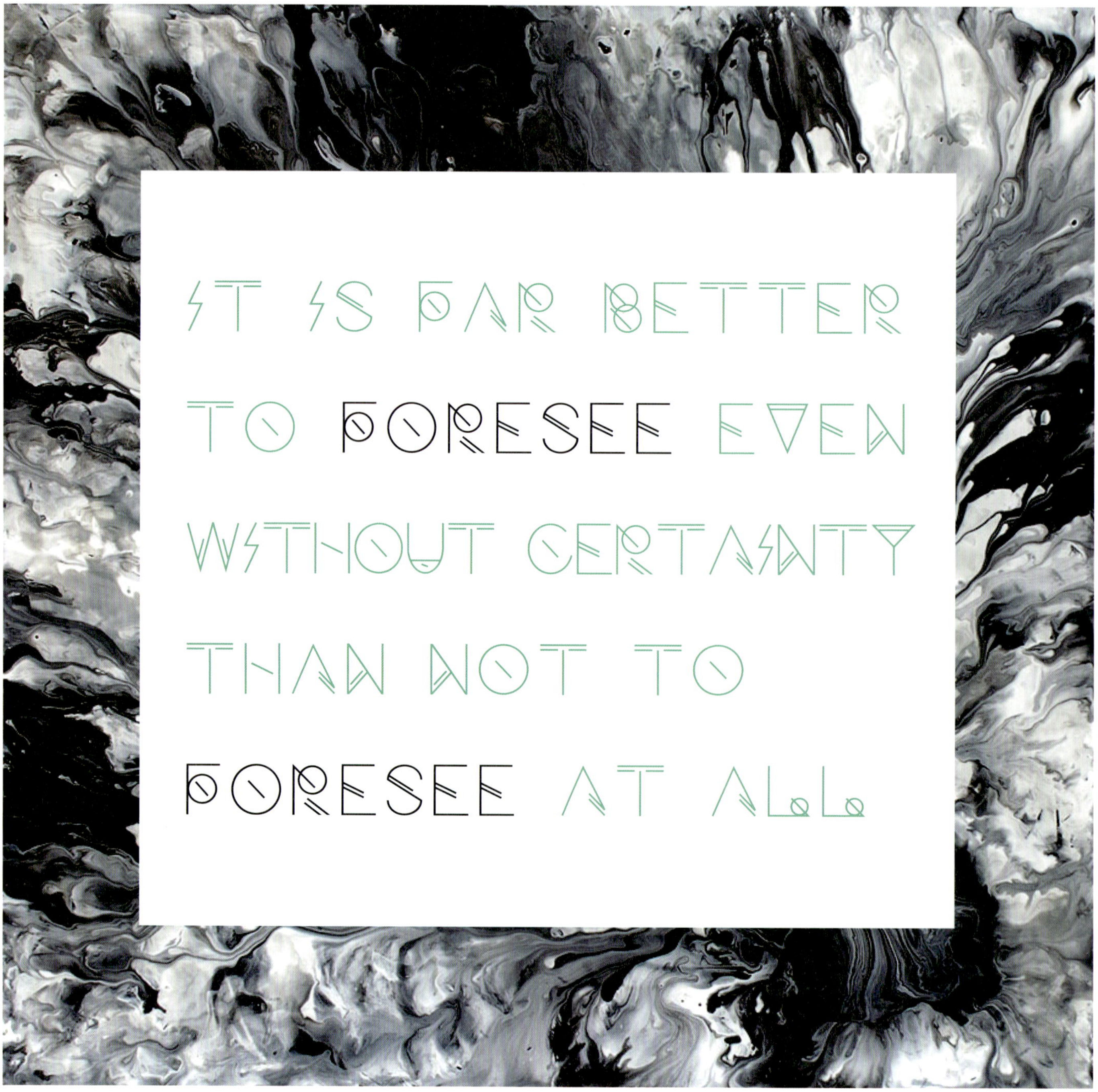

IT IS FAR BETTER
TO FORESEE EVEN
WITHOUT CERTAINTY
THAN NOT TO
FORESEE AT ALL

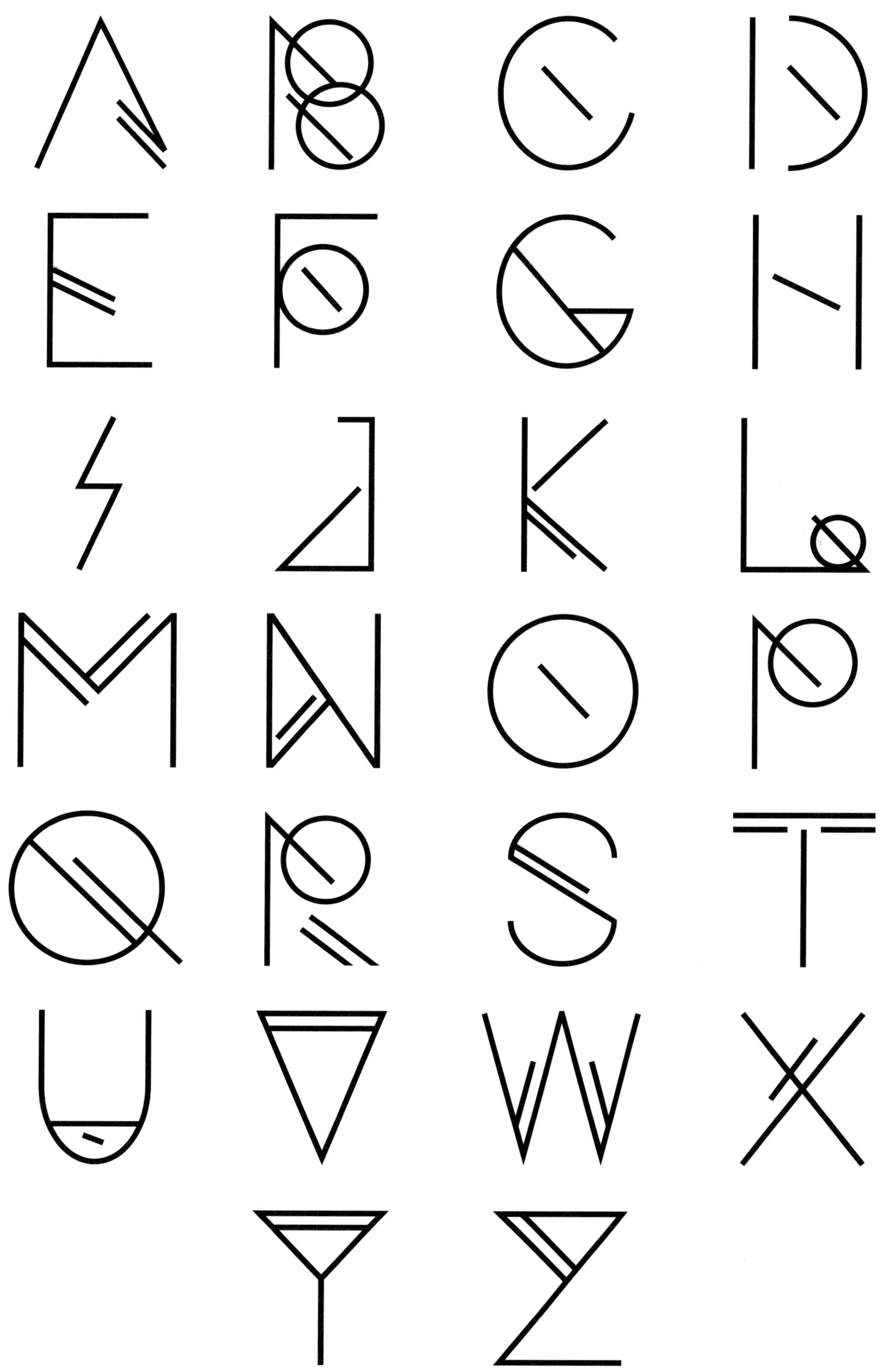

Multicolore Vector Font

Designer: Ivan Fllipov
Studio: neogrey creative

The designer has always been inspired by the logo design of Mohawk papers and produced this colorful Vector Font for everyone to create logo designs, posters and even some random art by overlapping different characters.

MULTICOLORE by neogrey creative

ABCDEFGH
IJKLMNOP
QRSTUVW
XYZ
1234567890
!?.,&%$€£

ĐŒÆØĄŁĘŻŹ
ČĆÇĞĬÍÌŇŃÑ
ÄĀÅÂÁÀÃĂ
ËĒE̊ÊÉÈẼĔ
ÖŌO̊ÔÓÒÕŎ
ÜŪŮÛÚÙŨŬ
ŸȲẙŶÝỲỸY̆

АБВГДЕЖЗ
ИЙКЛМН
ОПРСТУФХ
ЦЧЏШЩ
ЪЫЬЭЮЯ

MULTICOLORE by neogrey creative

Open the Layers Pallette and make **Color Set 2** for alternative colors and **Solid Thin** layer visible for additional effects

Latvia World Expo 2010

Designer: Asketic
Studio: Asketic

The designers have gone back to two basic elements of geometric shapes, the U shape and triangle. In deconstructing and rebuilding of these two shapes, a fresh image of the country has been formed and a new spirit of happiness has been ignited into Latvia's visual identity.

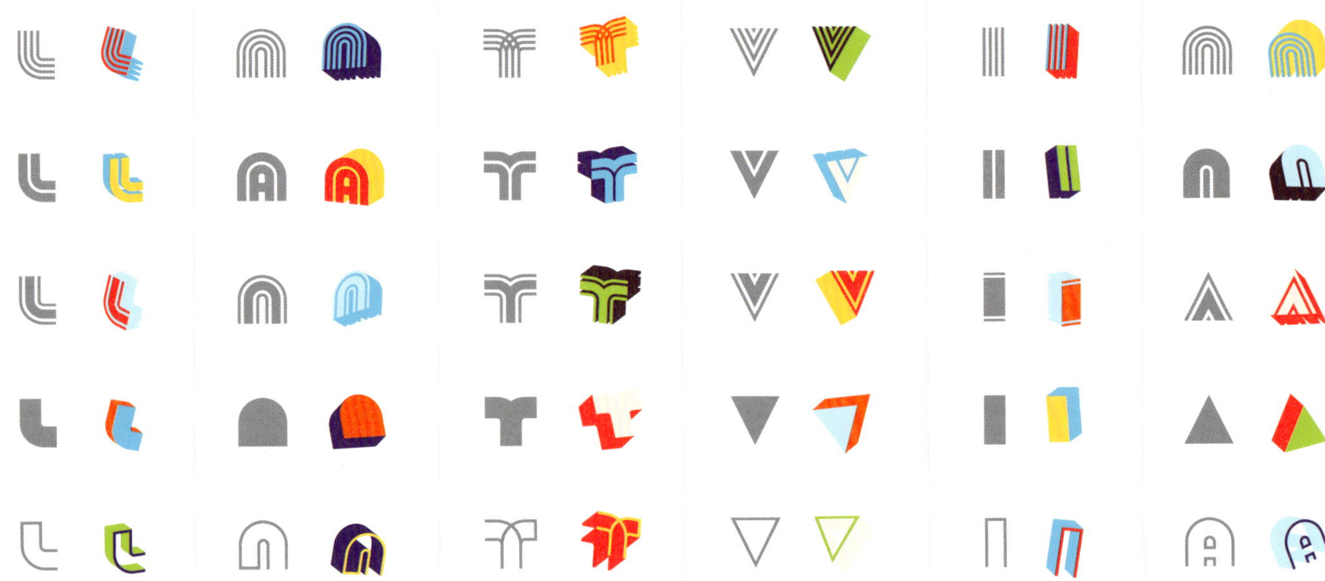

Latvia
EXPO 2010

Latvia
EXPO 2010

Latvia
EXPO 2010

Latvia
EXPO 2010

Latvia
EXPO 2010

Latvia
EXPO 2010

A B C D E F G H I

J K L M N O P Q R

S T U V W X Y Z

1 2 3 4 5 6 7 8 9 0

. , / % # @ * ( ) + – = "

< > : ; ! ? $ ^ [ ]

LATVIA PAVILION
EXPO 2010
TECHNOLOGY
OF HAPPINESS

ABCDEFGHI
JKLMNOPQR
STUVWXYZ
1234567890
. , / % # @ * ( ) + – = "
< > : ; ! ? $ ^ [ ]

XXII Blackened Wood

Designer: Lecter Johnson
Studio: Doubletwo Studios

XXII Blackened Wood is a font made for logo design or headlines in a book of magic spells. Its main shapes are results of black letter fonts compared with the decaying, organic look of roots or branches.

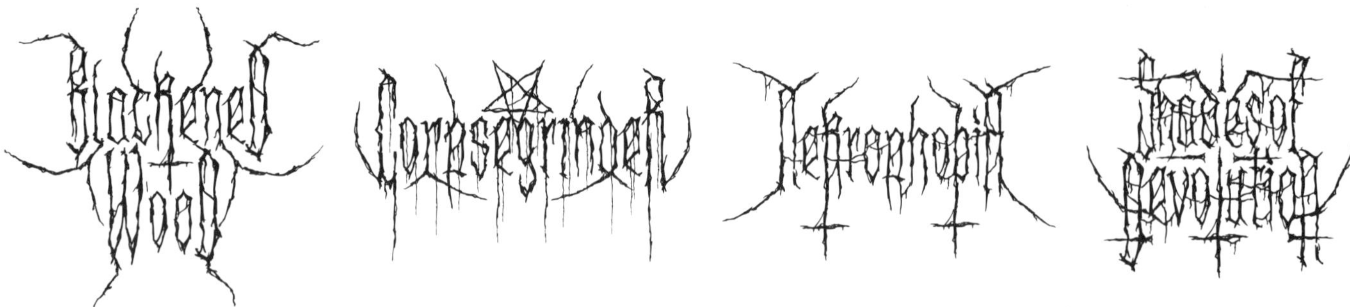

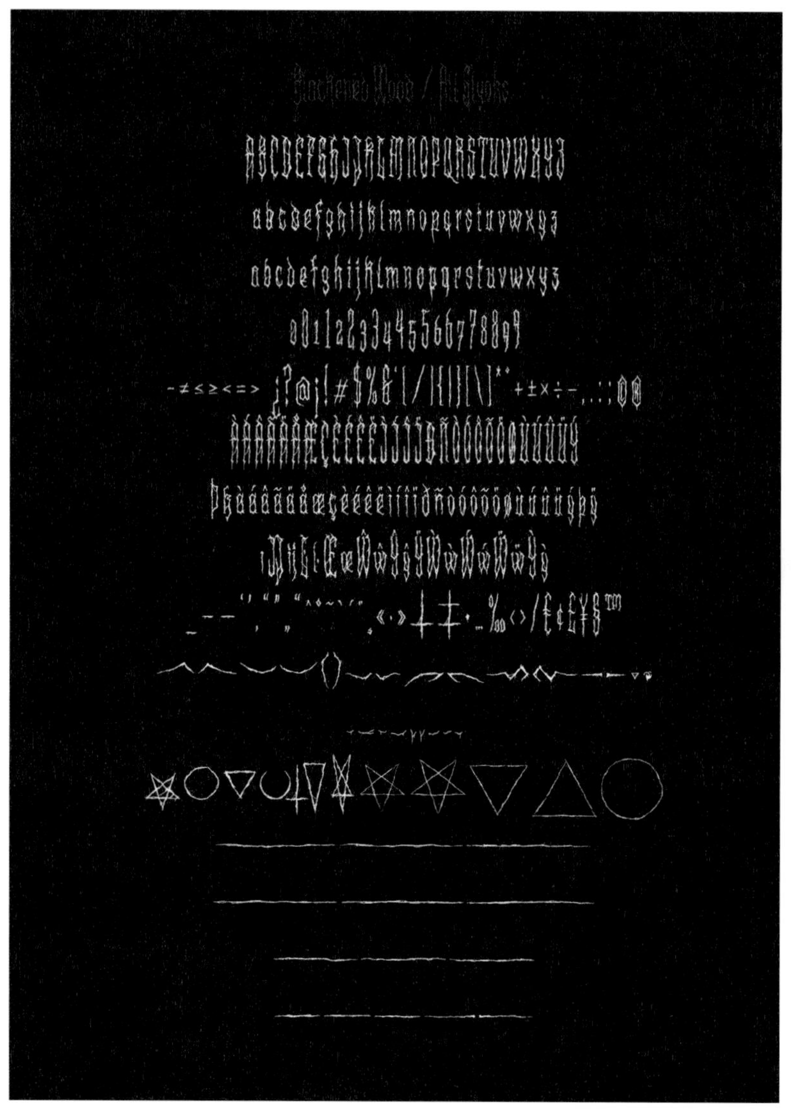

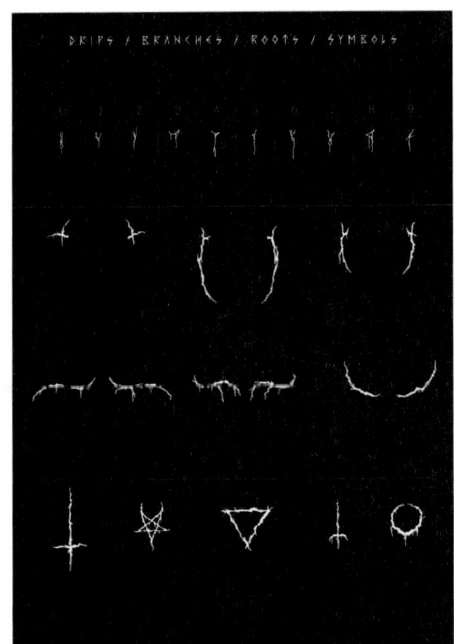

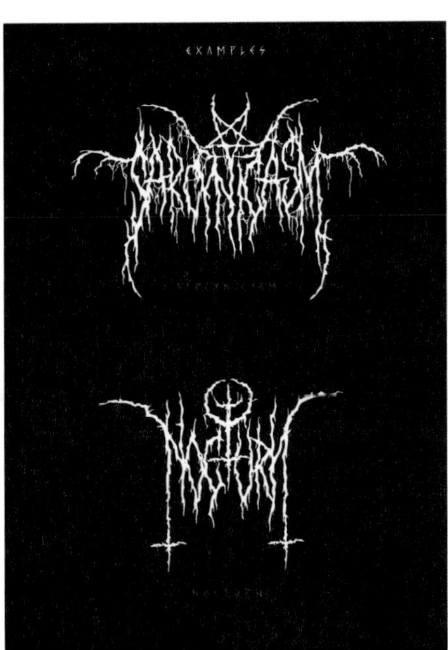

Corpsegrinder

OpenType

For detailed information about the „Black Magic Features" check out the PDF-File.

CHARACTERS

ABCDEFGHI
JKLMNOPQR
STUVWXYZ

ABCDEFGHI
JKLMNOPQR
STUVWXYZ

A B C D E F G H I J K L M N
O P Q R S T U V W X Y Z

aa bb cc dd ee ff gg hh ii
jj kk ll mm nn oo pp qq rr
ss tt uu vv ww xx yy zz

1 2 3 4 5 6 7 8 9 0
1 2 3 4 5 6 7 8 9 0

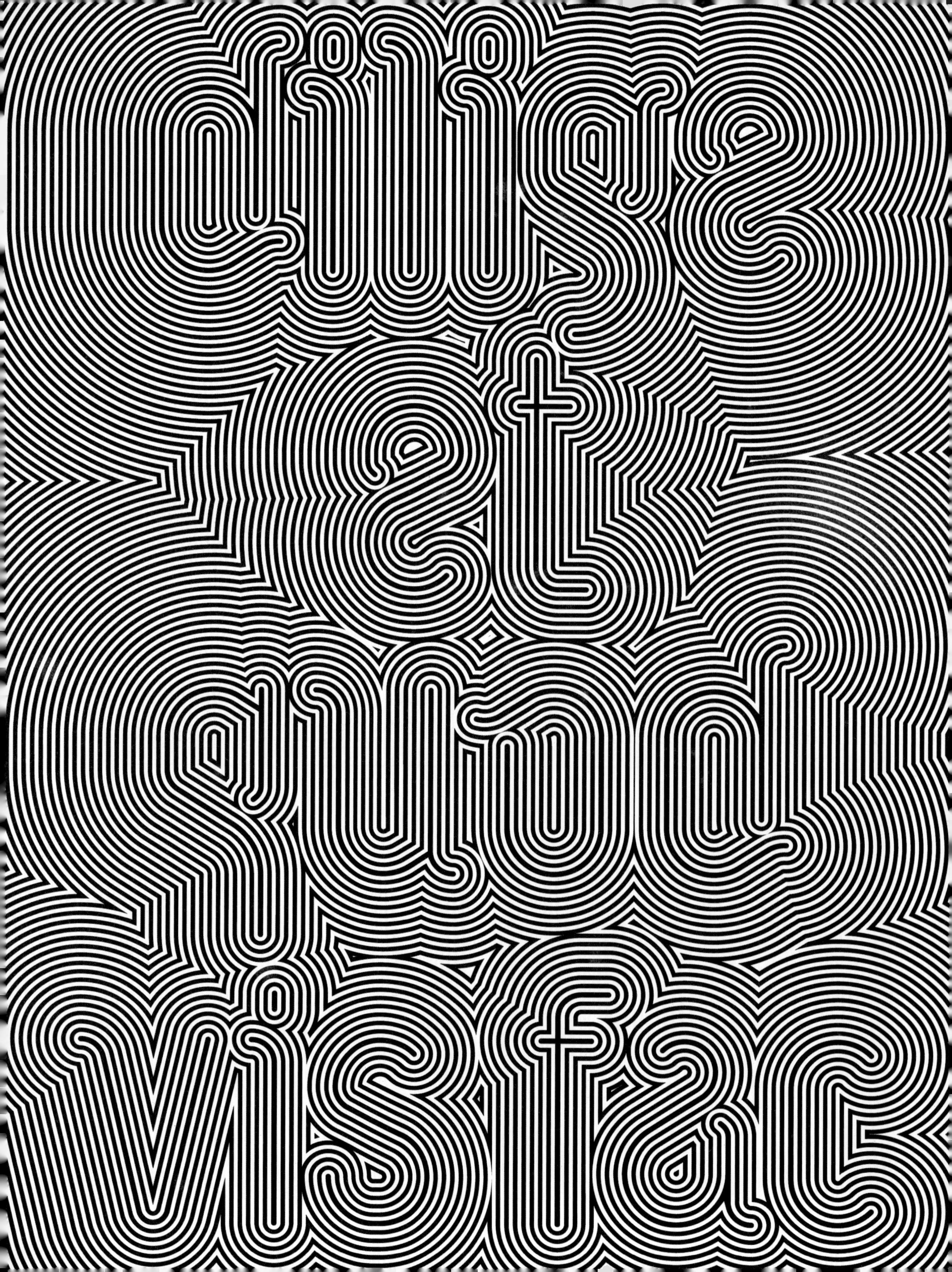

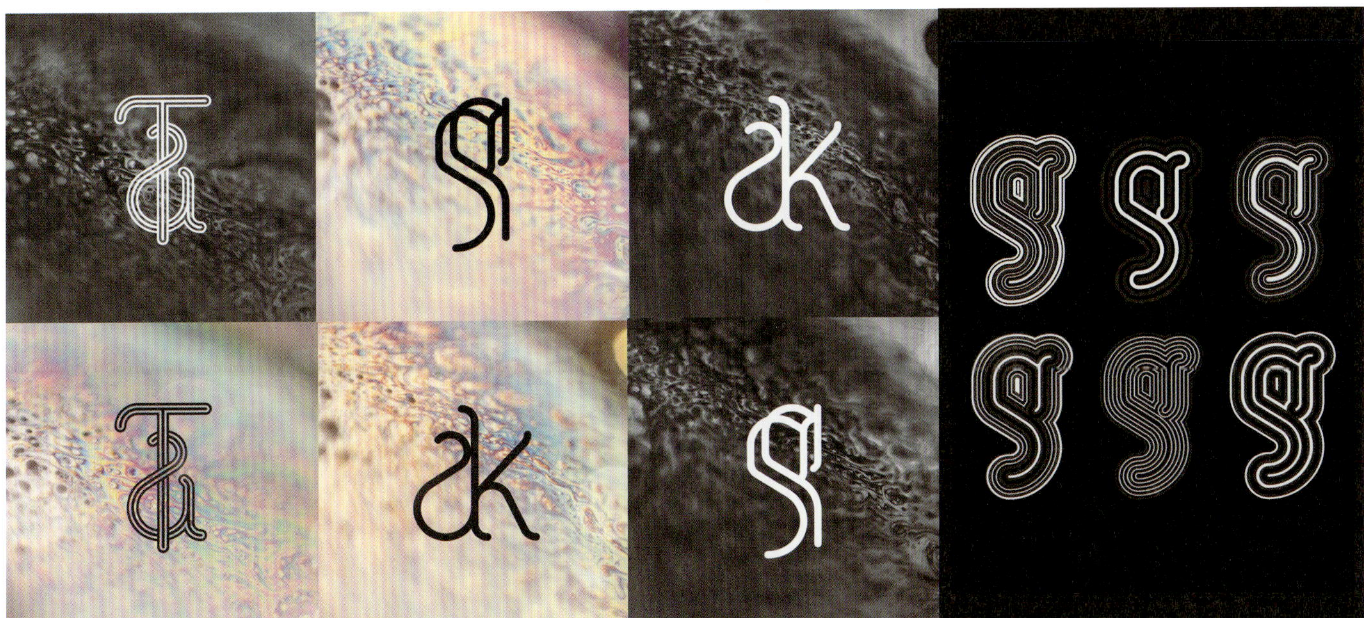

Vetka Type

Designer: Ruslan Khasanov

This typography is inspired by the Burmese alphabet with its open circular letters and natural forms, such as waves, horns and branches of trees which are reflected in the font as small sprouts and tails.

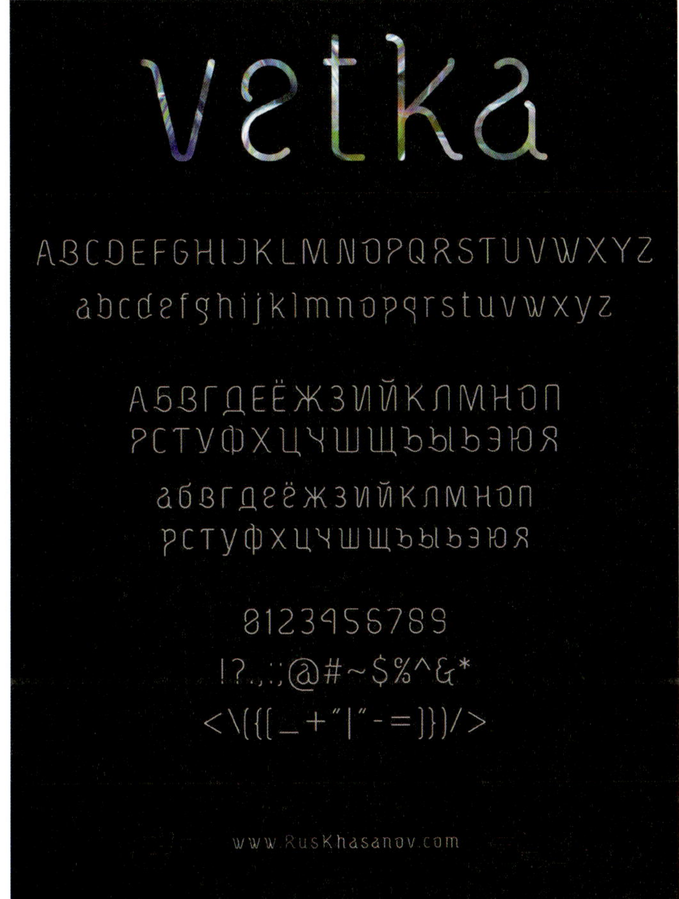

ETHNODRAMA,
LIVING THEATRE &
FORUM THEATRE
SERIES 1,2,3

人種誌戲劇生活劇場論壇劇場系列 1/2/3

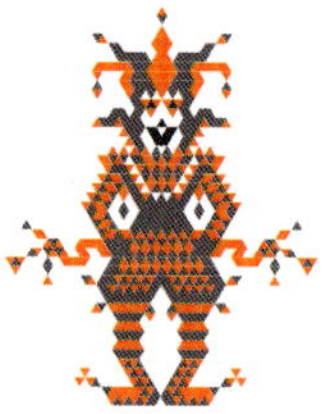

ACT MY LIFE
1/玩▲演▲完

CAN HELP, CAN HELP?!
2/幫到▲幫到?!

SHEEP WITH THE SKIN OF WOLVES
3/披著狼皮的羊

Ethnodrama

Designer: Benny Leung
Studio: STUDIO-M

Ethnodrama is a people-oriented drama education program which produced three performances by using three different theatrical techniques. In the main visual, the elements of facial expression and body movement were applied to the logotype design, making the whole project more dramatic.

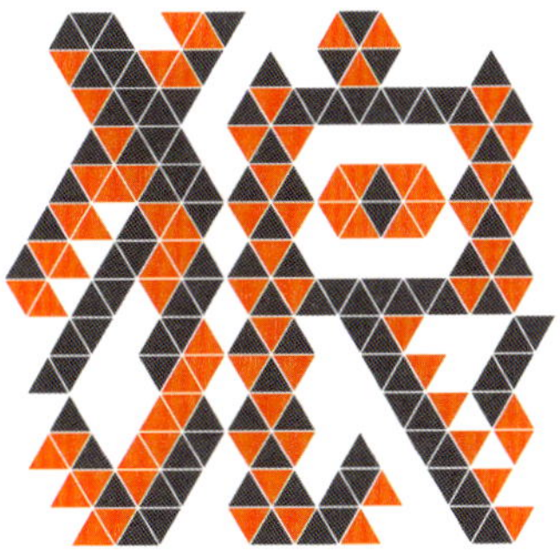

WOLF

FORUM

SHEEP

HELP

DRAMA

IDEAL

Free Tibet

Designer: Si Scott
Studio: Si Scott Studio Ltd.

The inspiration of the typeface originates from the temple of voice. The designer presented this idea by means of arranging meaningful words in strong contrast of colors while giving them a plain and smooth touch.

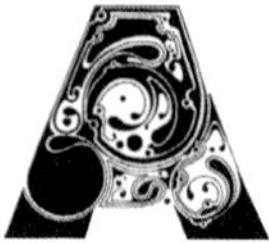

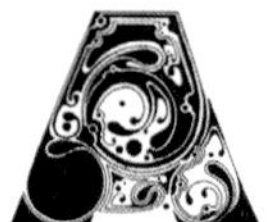

Embrace Typeface

Designer: Gareth Leyshon

The typeface is based on the idea of seamless patterns in which different shapes "embrace" each other in a confined space within letter forms.

Achille FY

Designer: Gregori Vincens, Gia Tran, Alisa Nowak,Bertrand Reguron & Valentine Proust
Studio: Fontyou

This Slab serif typeface is characterized by its curved and angular serifs. Its well balanced shapes make itself both legible in small size and powerful in big size for headlines.

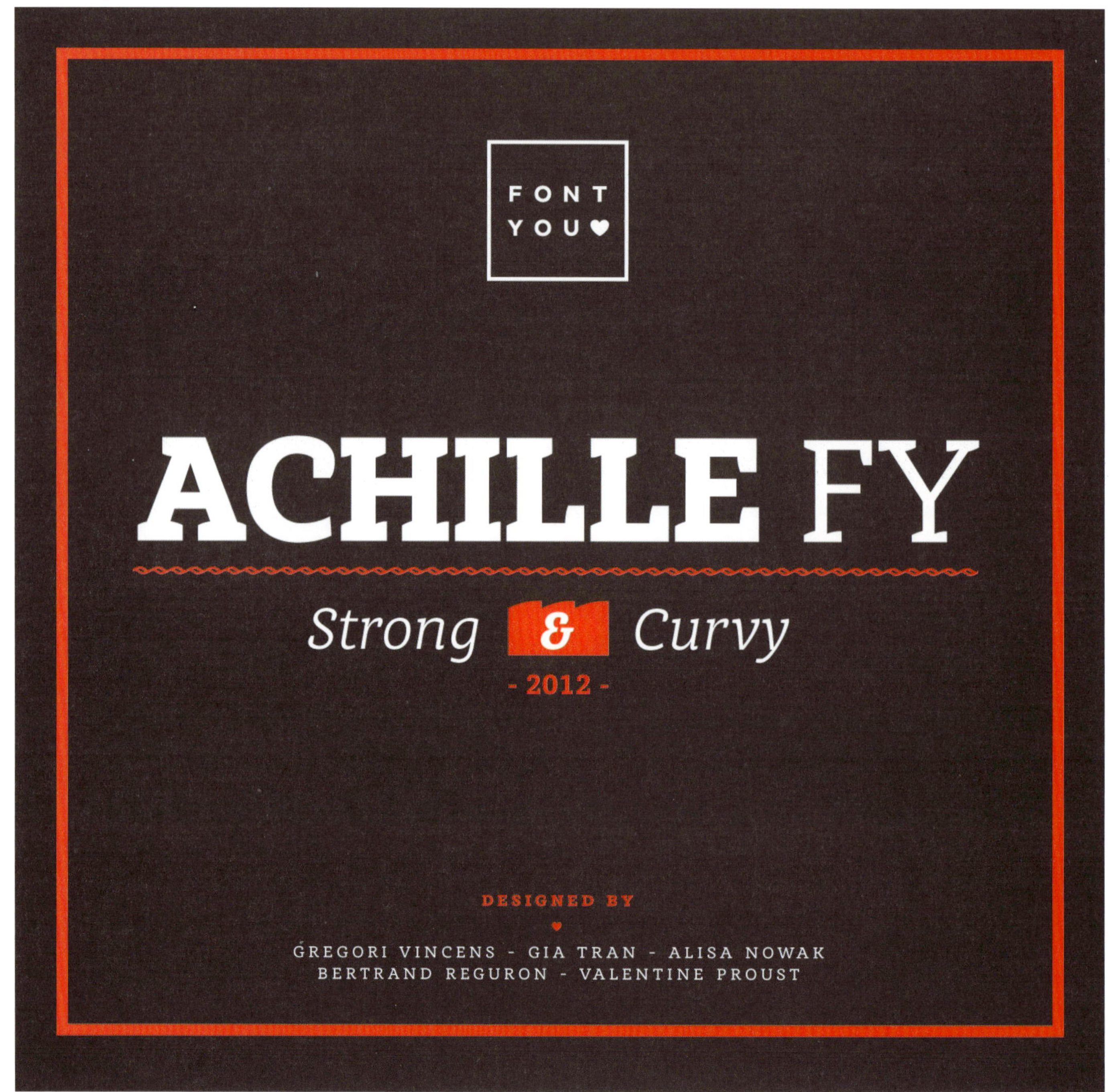

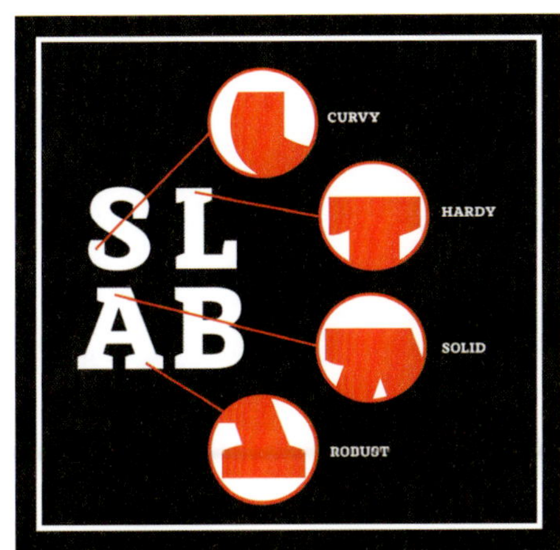

REGULAR CHARACTER SET

A B C D E F G H I J K L M N O P Q R S T U V W X Y Z [\ ] ^ _ ` a b
c d e f g h i j k l m n o p q r s t u v w x y z { | } ~ Ä Å Ç É Ñ Ö Ü
á à â ä ã å ç é è ê ë í ì î ï ñ ó ò ô ö õ ú ù û ü † ° ¢ £ § • ¶ ß ® ©
™ ´ ¨ ≠ Æ Ø ∞ ± ≤ ≥ ¥ µ ∂ ∑ ∏ π ∫ ª º Ω æ ø ¿ ¡ ¬ √ ƒ ≈ ∆ « » … À
Ã Õ Œ œ – — " " ' ' ÷ ◊ ÿ Ÿ / € ‹ › ﬁ ﬂ ‡ · ‚ „ ‰ Â Ê Á Ë È Í Î Ï Ì Ó Ô
Ò Ú Û Ù ı ˆ ˜ ¯ ˘ ˙ ˚ ¸ ˝ ˛ ˇ ! " # $ % & ' ( ) * + , - . / 0 1 2 3 4 5 6 7 8
9 : ; < = > ? @ i fb ffb fh ffh fj ffj fk ffk fi fi ft fft ffi ffl ♡ A B C D E
F G H I J K L M N O P Q R S T U V W X Y Z Æ Œ Ł Ø Đ Þ Ĳ A B C D E F
G H I J K L M N O P Q R S T U V W X Y Z Æ Œ Ł Ø Đ Þ Ĳ & ! ? ¡ ¿ ( ) { }
[ ] - , „ ' " ' " ' " I SS FI FL Á Ă Â Ä Ǽ À Ā Ą Å Ǻ Ã Ć Č Ç Ĉ Ċ Ď Đ É Ĕ Ě Ê
Ë Ė È Ē Ę Ğ Ĝ Ģ Ġ Ħ Ĥ Í Ĭ Î Ï İ Ì Ī Į Ĵ Ķ Ĺ Ľ Ļ Ŀ Ń Ň Ņ Ñ Ó Ŏ Ô Ö Ò Ő Ō Ǿ
Õ Ŕ Ř Ŗ Ś Š Ş Ŝ Ș Ŧ Ť Ţ Ț Ú Ŭ Û Ü Ù Ű Ū Ų Ů Ũ Ẃ Ŵ Ẅ Ẁ Ý Ŷ Ÿ Ỳ Ź Ž
Ż Á Ă Â Ä Ǽ À Ā Ą Å Ǻ Ã Ć Č Ç Ĉ Ċ Ď Đ É Ĕ Ě Ê Ë Ė È Ē Ę Ğ Ĝ Ģ Ġ Ħ
Ĥ Í Ĭ Î Ï İ Ì Ī Į Ĩ Ĵ Ķ Ĺ Ľ Ļ Ŀ Ń Ň Ņ Ñ Ó Ŏ Ô Ö Ò Ő Ō Ø Õ Ŕ Ř Ŗ Ś Š Ş Ŝ Ș
Ŧ Ť Ţ Ț Ú Ŭ Û Ü Ù Ű Ū Ų Ů Ũ Ẃ Ŵ Ẅ Ẁ Ý Ŷ Ÿ Ỳ Ź Ž Ż ı a b c d e f g h i
j k l m n o p q r s t u v w x y z è # € $ ¥ £ ¢ ƒ ¤ 0 1 2 3 4 5 6 7 8 9 # €
$ ¥ £ ¢ ƒ ¤ 0 1 2 3 4 5 6 7 8 9 # € $ ¥ £ ¢ ƒ ¤ 0 1 2 3 4 5 6 7 8 9 %
‰ ¤ ¦ - ² ³ ¹ ¼ ½ ¾ Đ × Ý Þ ð ý þ Ā ā Ă ă Ą ą Ć ć Ĉ ĉ Ċ ċ Č č Ď ď
Đ đ Ē ē Ĕ ĕ Ė ė Ę ę Ě ě Ĝ ĝ Ğ ğ Ġ ġ Ģ ģ Ĥ ĥ Ħ ħ Ĩ ĩ Ī ī Ĭ ĭ Į į İ Ĳ ĳ Ĵ ĵ
Ķ ķ Ĺ ĺ Ļ ļ Ľ ľ Ŀ ŀ Ł ł Ń ń Ņ ņ Ň ň Ō ō Ŏ ŏ Ő ő Ŕ ŕ Ŗ ŗ Ř ř Ś ś Ŝ ŝ Ş ş
Š š Ţ ţ Ť ť Ŧ ŧ Ũ ũ Ū ū Ŭ ŭ Ů ů Ű ű Ų ų Ŵ ŵ Ŷ ŷ Ź ź Ż ż Ž ž Ǻ ǻ Ǽ
ǽ Ǿ ǿ Ș ș Ț ț Ẁ ẁ Ẃ ẃ Ẅ ẅ Ỳ ỳ Ω – ♥ ‚ ff

Fugue

Creative Director: Stefan Sagmeister
Art Direction & Design: Jessica Walsh
Design: Pedro Sanches & Shy Inbar
Programmation: Pedro Sanches
Studio: Sagmeister & Walsh

The typeface sought to visualize ephemerality as well as to embody lineage and elegance in the sense of constant regeneration and evolution.

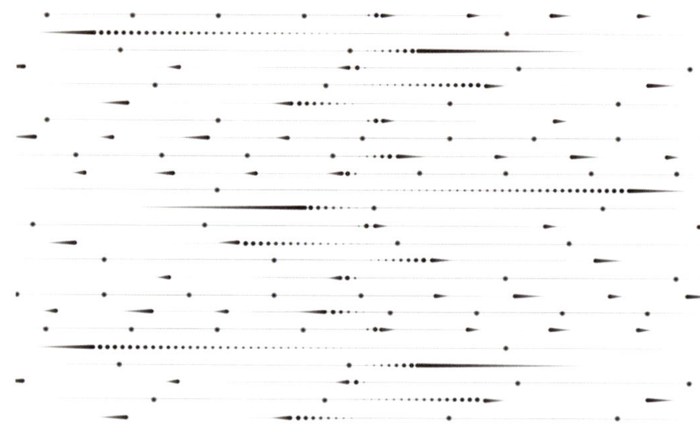

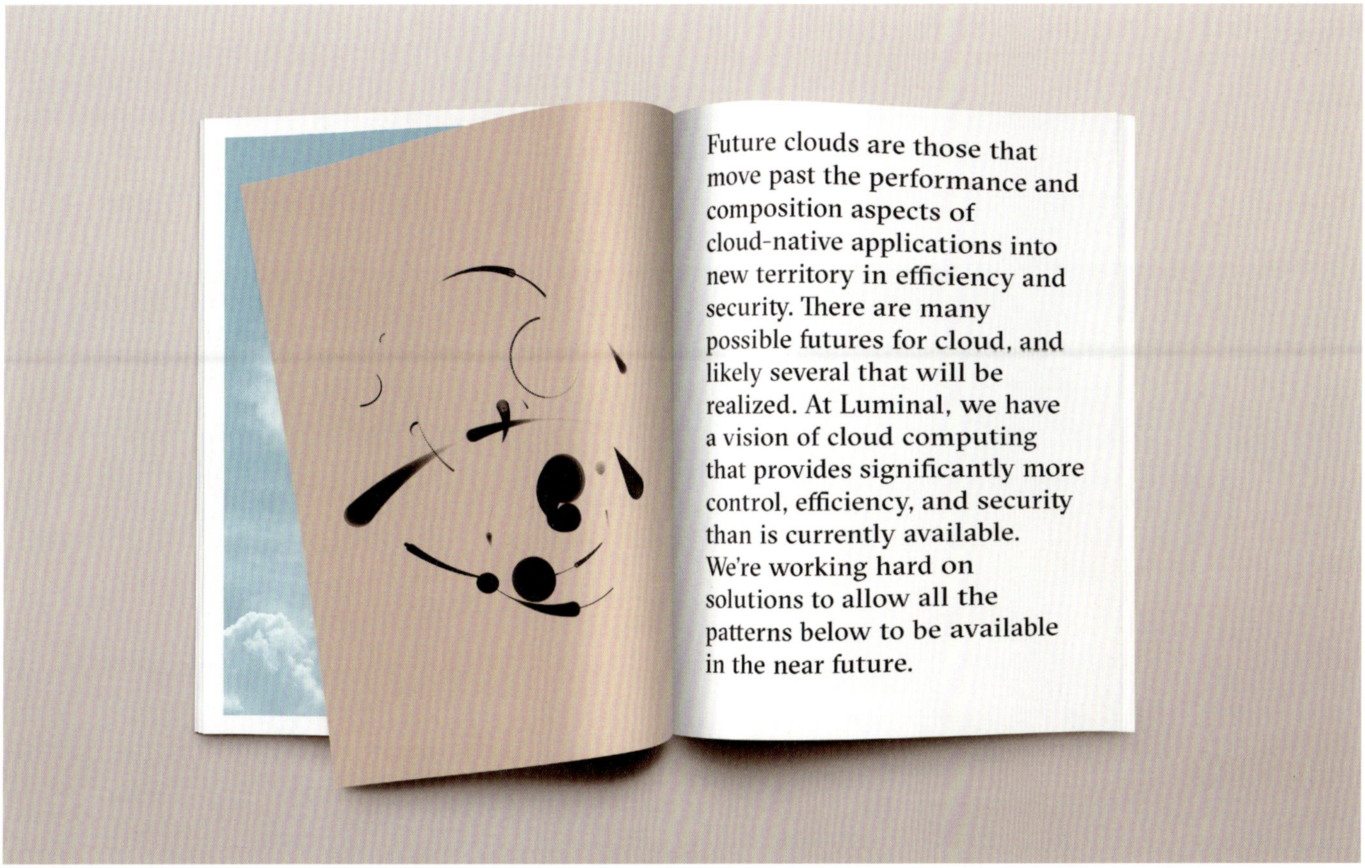

Future clouds are those that move past the performance and composition aspects of cloud-native applications into new territory in efficiency and security. There are many possible futures for cloud, and likely several that will be realized. At Luminal, we have a vision of cloud computing that provides significantly more control, efficiency, and security than is currently available. We're working hard on solutions to allow all the patterns below to be available in the near future.

RedBull Ginga Beat Radio

Designer: ALVA

This type design comes from the idea of making the musical feast a great hit scene and getting everybody moving. Therefore, the designer created a new identity for the project, which is strong on typographic attitude.

LUX
LISBOA
LIVE
RED BULL MUSIC ACADEMY RADIO
ON AIR
HUDSON MOHAWKE
LIVE
MARTYN
OCTA PUSH
PHOTONZ
VJ
SET
NO NAME
VIDEO
KASPAR

TEDxKowloon Salon 2013 AUG : IDEAL CITY

Designer: Benny Leung
Studio: STUDIO-M

Ideal and reality are often very different, but complementary. The typeface of the Chinese characters, meaning "ideal" and "you think", explains this philosophy of life.

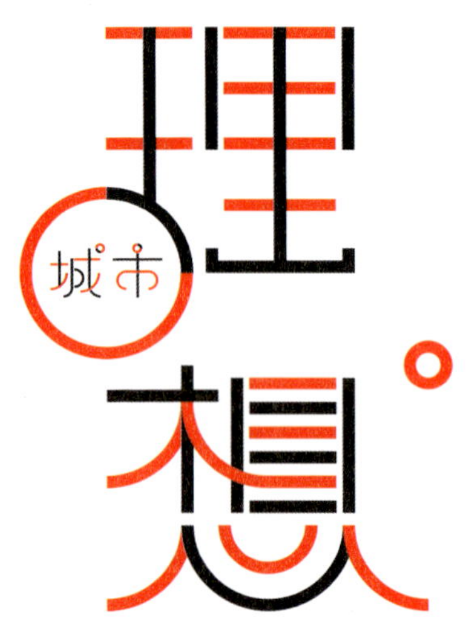

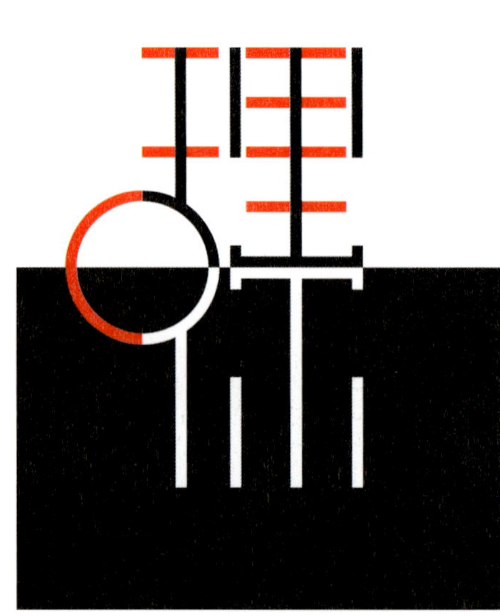

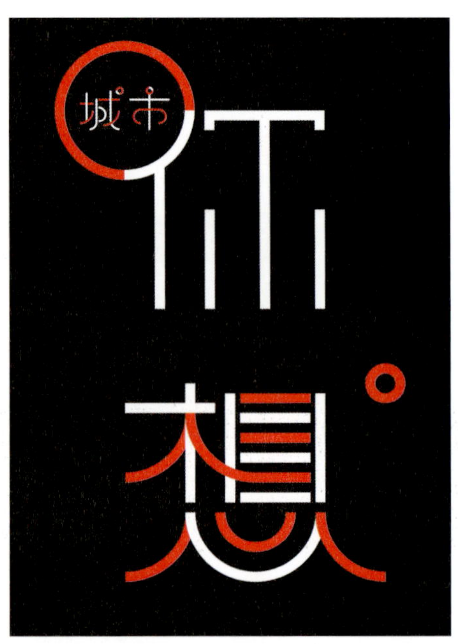

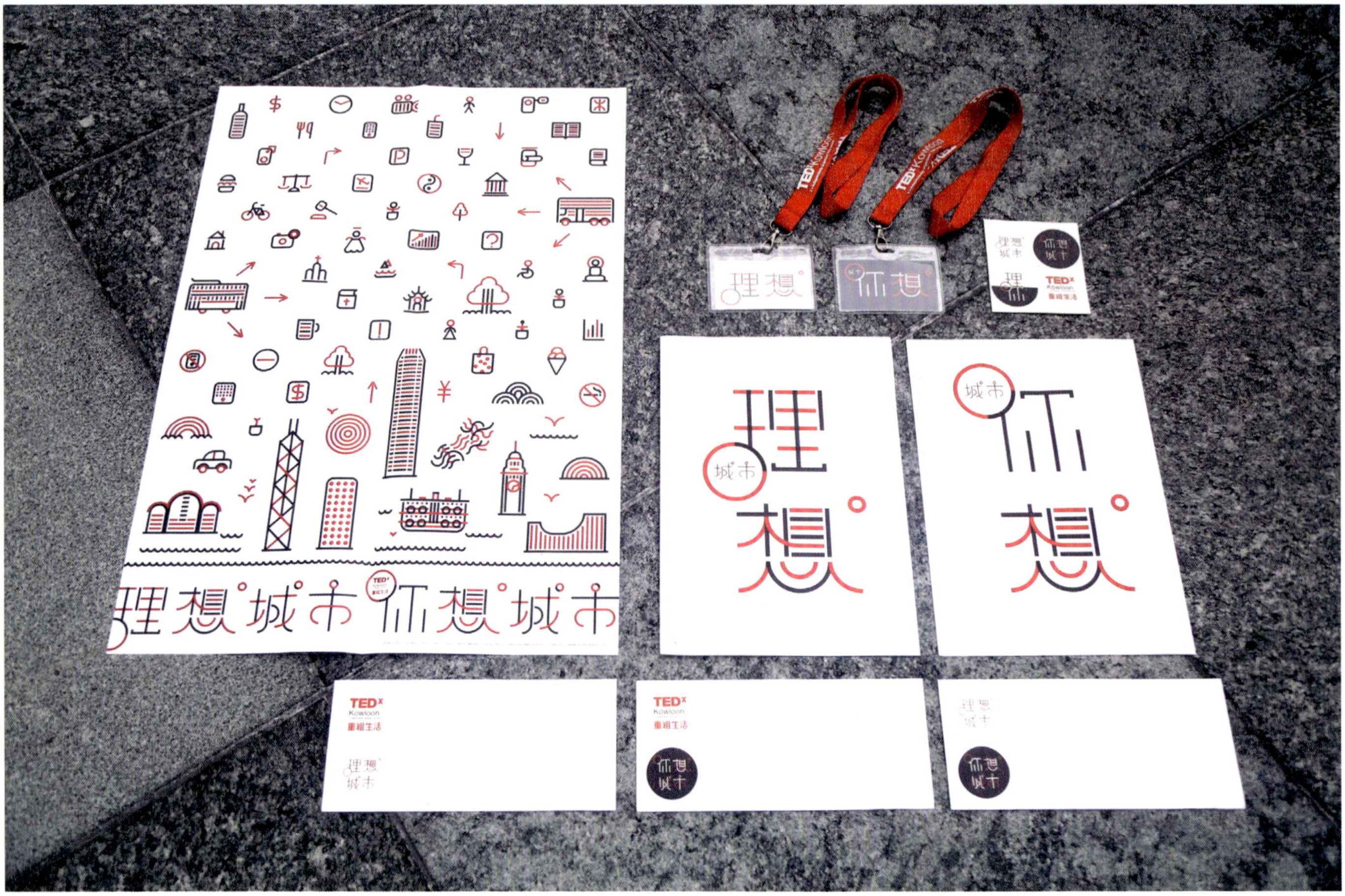

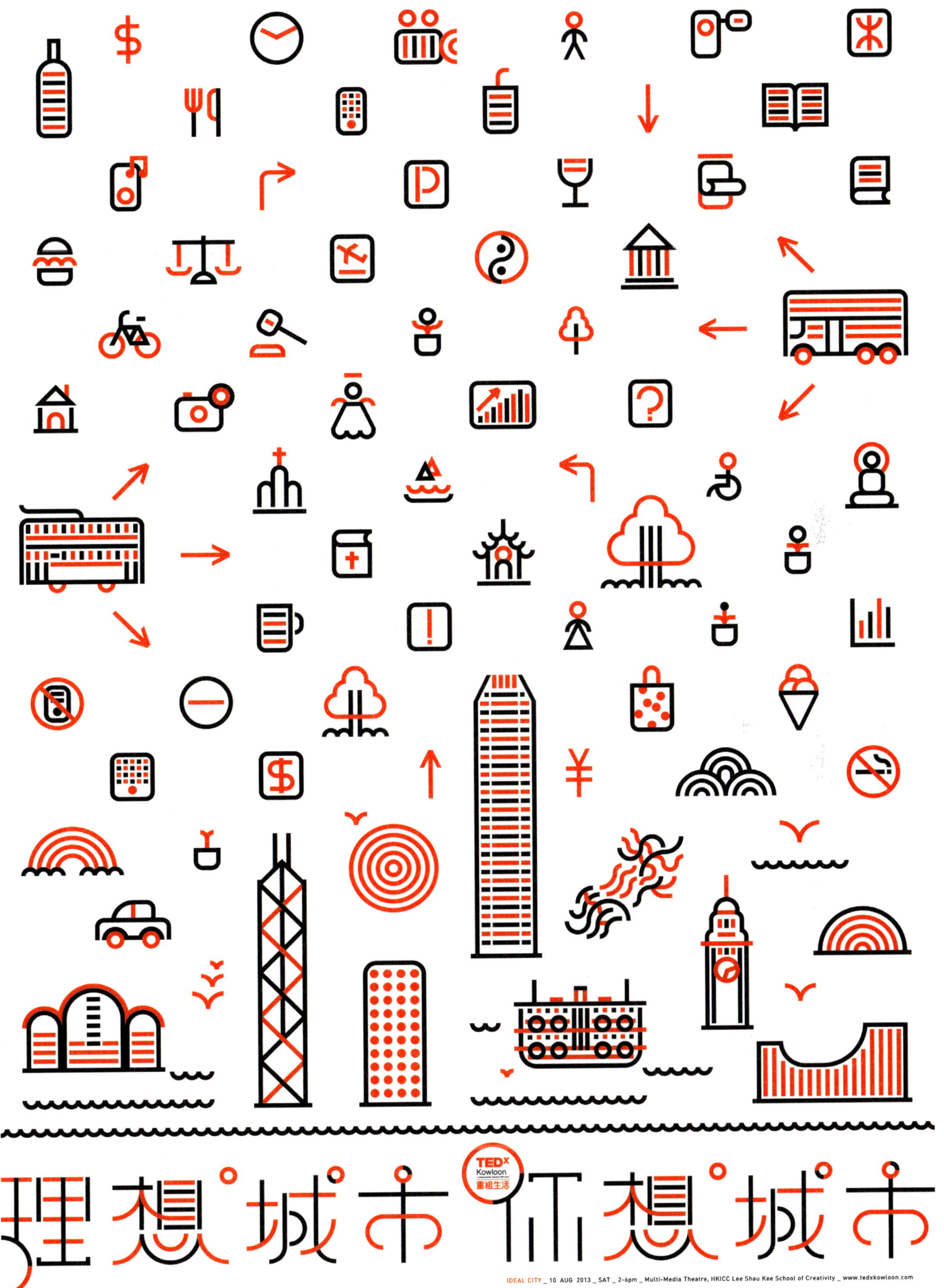
理想城市
TEDx Kowloon
重組生活
你想城市
IDEAL CITY _ 10 AUG 2013 _ SAT _ 2-6pm _ Multi-Media Theatre, HKICC Lee Shau Kee School of Creativity _ www.tedxkowloon.com

MESTIZO IS A TERM
TRADITIONALLY USED IN
LATIN AMERICA AND SPAIN
FOR PEOPLE OF MIXED
HERITAGE OR DESCENT.

IN SOME COUNTRIES IT
HAS COME TO MEAN A MIXTURE
OF EUROPEAN AND
AMERINDIAN.

MESTIZO LIKES:

TEQUILLA
JALAPEÑO
TACO TRUCKS
MEZCAL
ETHNO HIPSTERS
CHIPOTLES
&
FANDANGO CHICAS

MESTIZO

A VOLCANO TYPE FONT
BY JOHANNES KÖNIG

PLAY WITH
MESTIZO!

Mestizo

Studio: Melville Brand Design

The font Mestizo is based on a strict grid system of ethnic symbolism. Six weights can be combined in various ways. Accius, Alerio and Amias display the basic geometric shapes and Balbo, Belus and Borba represent the playful icons.

ABCDEFGHIJKLM
NOPQRSTUVWXYZ
?!ÄÖÜËŸ()/&ÀÁÂÃÅËÇŸ
1234567890*-+=/

MESTIZO ACCIUS

ABCDEFGHIJKLM
NOPQRSTUVWXYZ
?!ÄÖÜËŸ()/&ÀÁÂÃÅËÇŸ
1234567890*-+=/

MESTIZO ALERIO

ABCDEFGHIJKLM
NOPQRSTUVWXYZ
?!ÄÖÜËŸ<>/&ÀÁÂÃÅËÇŸ
1234567890*-+=/

MESTIZO AMIAS

ABCDEFGHIJKLM
NOPQRSTUVWXYZ
?!ÄÖÜËŸ()/&ÀÁÂÃÅËÇŸ
1234567890*-+=/

MESTIZO BALBO

ABCDEFGHIJKLM
NOPQRSTUVWXYZ
?!ÄÖÜËŸ()/&ÀÁÂÃÅËÇŸ
1234567890*-+=/

MESTIZO BELUS

ABCDEFGHIJKLM
NOPQRSTUVWXYZ
?!ÄÖÜËŸ<>/&ÀÁÂÃÅËÇŸ
1234567890*-+=/

MESTIZO BORBA

Hacking Habitat— Art of Control

Studio: Autobahn

The typeface is constructed by overlapping two parts: the Arial Black, which is a very basic, stern and constructed typeface, and the Times New Roman Bold, a typeface less constructed, more curved and with beautiful details. All sorts of colors were used to make each letter individual and different from each other.

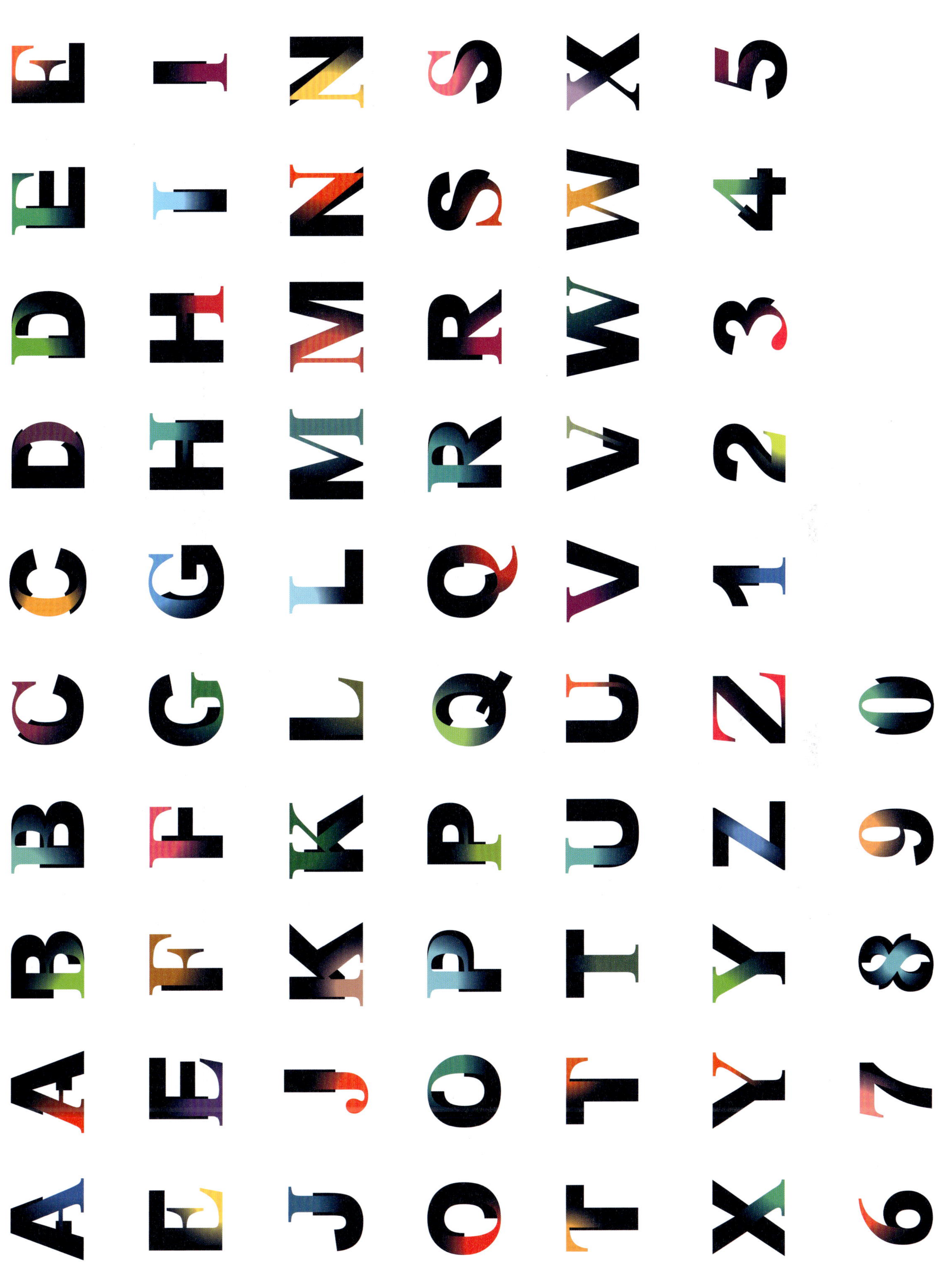

EXODUS

Designer: Beomyoung Sohn

Inspired by the decision tree, the most basic structure of Artificial Intelligence programming, the designer combined this special narrative form with the structure of a maze to talk about a story of sexual harassment which was experienced by his female friend.

Do I want to go outside for refreshments?
Y
N
Start to arrange the room.
Start
Take a walk.
My room is too messy.
Start
Start to work.
There is a house with an open window.
Is there a girl inside?
Stay
Someone is watching me through the window in the bathroom
Climb up the fence and peep at her.
Do I want to peep at her?
Too many accidents are happening.
Close the window and cry.
She closes the window and cries.
Hide and wait for 10 minutes near her home.
Do I need help?
Y
N
Call any police man on duty.
Does a police man arrive at her home?
Receive the report about very dangerous sexual harassment from a woman.
Call the police.
I can't stand my sexual desire.
Is there a police man to send?
He gets through the window and rapes me.
Get through the window and rape her.
Decide to move out.
Send a police man to her.
Stay at home with the police man until I feel safe.
Next Morning
Goal
Satisfy my sexual desire and return home safely.
Is it safe living in this house?
N
Y
Goal
Keep citizens safe.
Goal
Live in a safe house.
Her Nightmare with Two Perverts and Police
Terminal
Input / Output
Decision

Make a Data With Me

Designer: Gareth Leyshon

This typeface design comes from the idea of recording the words and phrases of passengers on a train journey from Cardiff to Neath.

I TYPE TO SAY

Among all those graphic elements, there are a bunch of people who specifically put their heart and soul into designing typefaces for years and years, and they are still enjoying it nonetheless. From the most classic and renown typefaces, such as Helvetica and Times New Roman, to today's diverse creations of typefaces, these people keep expand their boundaries while embracing the development of digitization. What do they think of the trend of typeface design? How do they balance the artistic pursuit and business needs? Features and interviews followed will reveal to you the inner thoughts of a typeface designer.

Helvetica

I TYPE TO SAY

Times New Roman

Digitization of Typeface

Classic VS Modern

"Classic" and "Modern" are two concepts related to both time and style. Styles could be reflected through fonts or typefaces applied in graphic design. Generally, classic style is mostly manifested in an ornate and relatively complicated form, communicating cultural, emotional or traditional messages; while modern style tends to be represented in a simple, rational, individualized and functional expression. All these qualities can be found in every stroke of a font or a typeface.

In typography, serif typeface refers to fonts with tails, flags and feet, which is decorative, readable and handwriting-featured; and it has been frequently linked to tradition and the old times and meanwhile represents a classic style. For example, for Latin or Roman alphabet, typical serif typefaces include Times New Roman, Garamond and Palationo. With regard to Chinese characters, Songti, Official Script, Ximingti are all serif typefaces. In contrast, sans serif is often used to depict modern style, characterized without tails, flags or feet, with simpler, modern and minimal forms, like Arial, Tahoma and Verdana for Latin alphabet, and SIMYOU for Chinese characters. Since eclectic style has become prevailing in the 20th century, typeface design was combined with multiple theories, approaches and forms for various demands. Therefore, to distinguish the classic-style typeface from a modern-style one based on featuring serif or not is not sufficient enough. Yet, to some extent, this classification works sometimes when we refer to typeface applications of the past.

Although the approaches to typeface design are different from one another, there are some general processing manners that could be summarized when designers are creating a certain typeface with a classic or modern style. For classic style, involving serif, vintage, decorative elements or signs with historical significance in the typeface is a good way. When it comes to modern style, designers can adopt the expression of minimalism, geometry and Bauhaus, etc. No matter what method is applied, the key point is to keep the overall style of the typeface consistent so as to merge into the whole design, especially for branding.

Form and function are crucial to design, but they are not the only indicator; to build an emotional connection with the audience through brands has become the most urgent demand nowadays. That's why the combination of classic and modern style in typeface design has become a trend. It is necessary to integrate cultural and emotional elements with calm, minimal and functional modern design through typography presentation which conveys brand information, image and marketing.

Whether designers choose a font or design a customized font for a brand, the fonts should be integrated with the brand personality. Fonts themselves communicate certain qualities. Only if the fonts used convey similar vibes with brands and are unified, whether they are applied in logo, signage, catalog and so forth, could the fonts present the expected image. In this feature, we will lead you into how typeface designers and brand designers think about integrating classic and modern style into typeface design and how typeface becomes a useful tool to reflect brand traits through interviews with Western typeface designers and Chinese character designers.

Legendary Type - Helvetica

Some said, “If you are not sure which Western typeface to use, just pick Helvetica.” You can see how influential and legendary it is from this saying. Walking along the street, you might see various signboards using Helvetica. Actually, many large, multinational companies use Helvetica as their business typeface. In brief, Helvetica is ubiquitous. But how much do you know about it ?

Helvetica is a sans serif typeface, created in Switzerland of 1957. This was a time when manual type-setting was a mainstream in Switzerland. But people were longing for a more pragmatic and international typeface style. Therefore, when Helvetica came out with its practicability and adaptability, it became a great hit at once.

Helvetica was designed by Max Midinger and Eduard Hoffmann. Midinger was a marketing consultant who understood the market and clients’ needs and he’s also a typeface designer, which was exactly what Hoffmann asked for. Hoffmann, on the other hand, was practical and familiar with business management. Midinger and Hoffmann didn’t confine themselves. They modestly consulted their predecessors and peers in order to adjust the design direction and details, eventually making Helvetica enjoying the largest group of users.

All these factors - the historical background, adaptable style, tacit cooperation and accurate analysis of market - made it legendary. Legend cannot be duplicated. We can only hope for the next one to come.

ABCDEFabcdef

ABCDEFabcdef

ABCDEFabcdef

ABCDEFabcdef

ABCDEFabcdef

ABCDEFabcdef

ABCDEFabcdef

ABCDEFabcdef

Legendary Type
-
Times New Roman

If Helvetica is the legend of sans serif, then the most well known serif would be Times New Roman. When you use a word processor to type English words, you are most likely to see Times New Roman which is so commonly used that people usually forget about how great it is.

Times New Roman is a serif typeface created in 1932 by Monotype. It is quite an anecdote speaking of the creation process. At the beginning, typeface designer from Monotype, Stanley Morison, mocked that Times had an outdated typeface. In response, Times challenged him to design a better typeface. Stanley Morison accepted the challenge. With the help of another two designers, Victor Lardent and Starling Burgess, he perfectly designed this serif featured with durability and ancient letter style.

When it comes to the reasons of its success, apart from being so standard that many computer programs set it as the default font; more importantly, it earned its popularity along with the spread of Times. Many American publishers began to purchase the right to use Times New Roman: in 1941, Times New Roman welcomed its biggest American client; in 1953, Chicago Sun-Times began to adopt Times New Roman as their printing typeface. Although later on Times no longer used this typeface, it is non-stoppable that Times New Roman has become a classic typeface that is not only loved and known, but also influences future typeface design and sets an precedent of newspaper owning its particular typeface.

ABCDEFabcdef

ABCDEFabcdef

ABCDEFabcdef

ABCDEFabcdef

ABCDEFabcdef

ABCDEFabcdef

ABCDEFabcdef

ABCDEFabcdef

Digitization of Typeface

People's access to information is constantly changing towards digitization which evolves from the earlier platforms like television and PC to mobile phone and tablet. The typeface design industry has new problems to solve: how to better adjust to hand printing, how to transform the making process to fit in with machine printing, and ultimately how to maximize readability in electronic devices. The coming out of Apple Watch brings up more challenges to typeface design.

Monotype has developed a software for small screen typeface which can be used in smart watch and dashboard and can present the same experience and quality to users as in large screen. However, the small screen typeface's pixel is decreased if zoomed up. Moreover, behind the electronic devices is the amazing Internet full of rapidly changing information, which typeface has to be capable of presenting. Since the information is unpredictable and whether users are using the large or small screen is unknown, typeface ought to prepare for the coming challenge. Grid systems are no longer fit for the trend of dimensional typeface presentation. The presentation of typeface including the size is decided by readers who choose in accordance with their preferences. Mark Boulton, the pioneer of responsive design, has said in a published article: "To design a web typeface that fits for presenting content in every device, we need to abandon old concepts of graphic design. What we need to do is to create designs that can be used in all electronic devices."

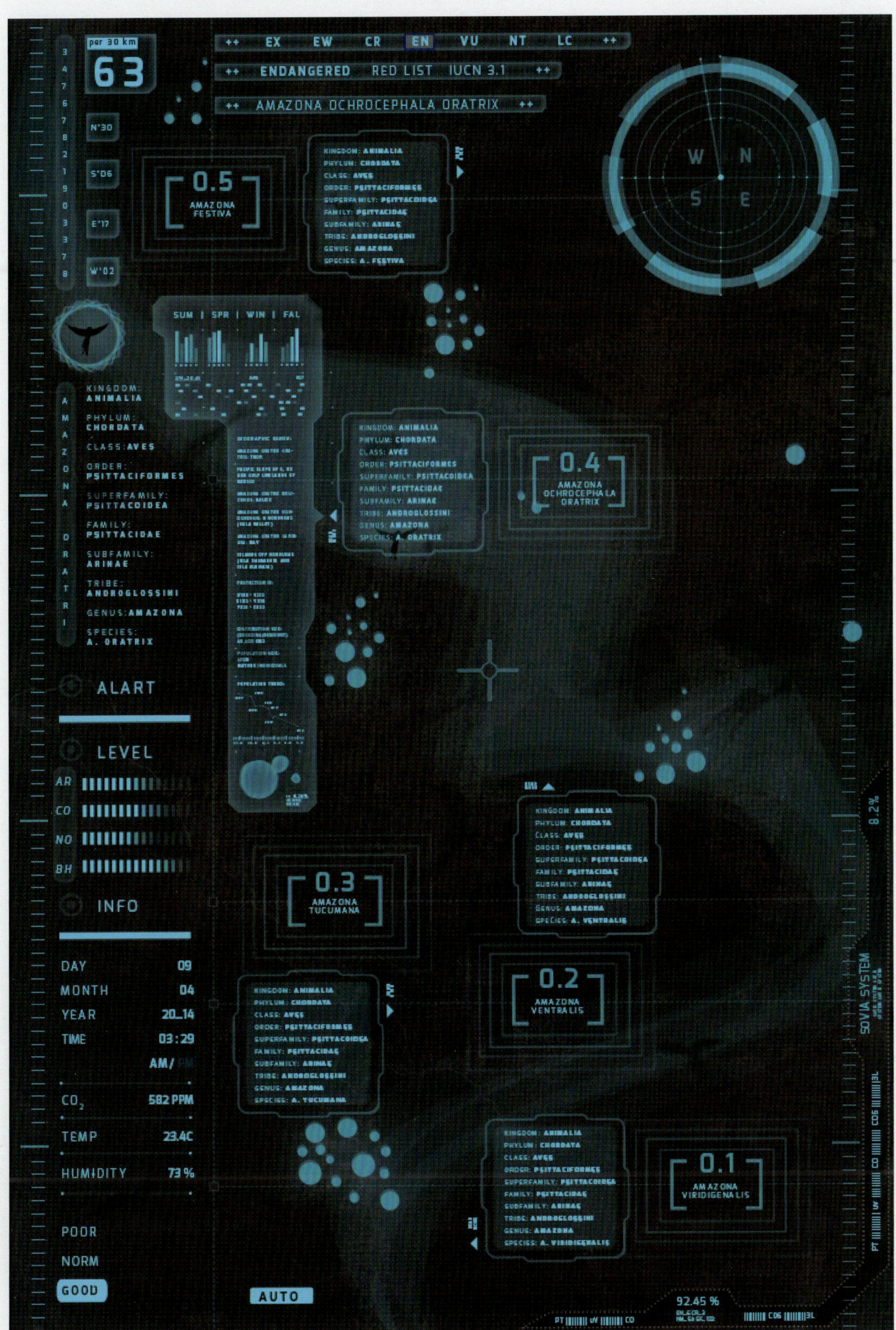
per 30 km
63
N°30
S°06
E°17
W°02
++ EX EW CR EN VU NT LC ++
++ ENDANGERED RED LIST IUCN 3.1 ++
++ AMAZONA OCHROCEPHALA ORATRIX ++
0.5
AMAZONA FESTIVA
KINGDOM: ANIMALIA
PHYLUM: CHORDATA
CLASS: AVES
ORDER: PSITTACIFORMES
SUPERFAMILY: PSITTACOIDEA
FAMILY: PSITTACIDAE
SUBFAMILY: ARINAE
TRIBE: ANDROGLOSSINI
GENUS: AMAZONA
SPECIES: A. FESTIVA
W N S E
SUM | SPR | WIN | FAL
KINGDOM: ANIMALIA
PHYLUM: CHORDATA
CLASS: AVES
ORDER: PSITTACIFORMES
SUPERFAMILY: PSITTACOIDEA
FAMILY: PSITTACIDAE
SUBFAMILY: ARINAE
TRIBE: ANDROGLOSSINI
GENUS: AMAZONA
SPECIES: A. ORATRIX
KINGDOM: ANIMALIA
PHYLUM: CHORDATA
CLASS: AVES
ORDER: PSITTACIFORMES
SUPERFAMILY: PSITTACOIDEA
FAMILY: PSITTACIDAE
SUBFAMILY: ARINAE
TRIBE: ANDROGLOSSINI
GENUS: AMAZONA
SPECIES: A. ORATRIX
0.4
AMAZONA OCHROCEPHALA ORATRIX
ALART
LEVEL
AR
CO
NO
BH
INFO
DAY 09
MONTH 04
YEAR 20_14
TIME 03:29
AM/PM
CO2 582 PPM
TEMP 23.4C
HUMIDITY 73 %
POOR
NORM
GOOD
0.3
AMAZONA TUCUMANA
KINGDOM: ANIMALIA
PHYLUM: CHORDATA
CLASS: AVES
ORDER: PSITTACIFORMES
SUPERFAMILY: PSITTACOIDEA
FAMILY: PSITTACIDAE
SUBFAMILY: ARINAE
TRIBE: ANDROGLOSSINI
GENUS: AMAZONA
SPECIES: A. VENTRALIS
0.2
AMAZONA VENTRALIS
KINGDOM: ANIMALIA
PHYLUM: CHORDATA
CLASS: AVES
ORDER: PSITTACIFORMES
SUPERFAMILY: PSITTACOIDEA
FAMILY: PSITTACIDAE
SUBFAMILY: ARINAE
TRIBE: ANDROGLOSSINI
GENUS: AMAZONA
SPECIES: A. TUCUMANA
KINGDOM: ANIMALIA
PHYLUM: CHORDATA
CLASS: AVES
ORDER: PSITTACIFORMES
SUPERFAMILY: PSITTACOIDEA
FAMILY: PSITTACIDAE
SUBFAMILY: ARINAE
TRIBE: ANDROGLOSSINI
GENUS: AMAZONA
SPECIES: A. VIRIDIGENALIS
0.1
AMAZONA VIRIDIGENALIS
AUTO
92.45 %
8.2%
SOVIA SYSTEM

INTERVIEW WITH

Benoît Bodhuin

Typography Designer

Benoît Bodhuin is a French designer, specializing in graphic design and typography. Pursuing his occupation for ten years, his work includes personal projects and business designs.

▶ What do you think about the relationship between design styles and typography?

From the point of view of typography, the style follows the historical evolution of typography: turnaround of the axis, geometrization and sans serif in advertising and display, etc. From the perspective of design, it seems more complicated: since the early 20th century, graphic currents follow one after another (Art Nouveau, Dada, Bauhaus, Swiss style, psychedelism, etc.,) and it is not easy to identify a trend. However, if we consider that the legacy of the Swiss style is currently predominant then we can identify some trends like rationalization, organization, geometric associated with the use of grotesque typefaces.

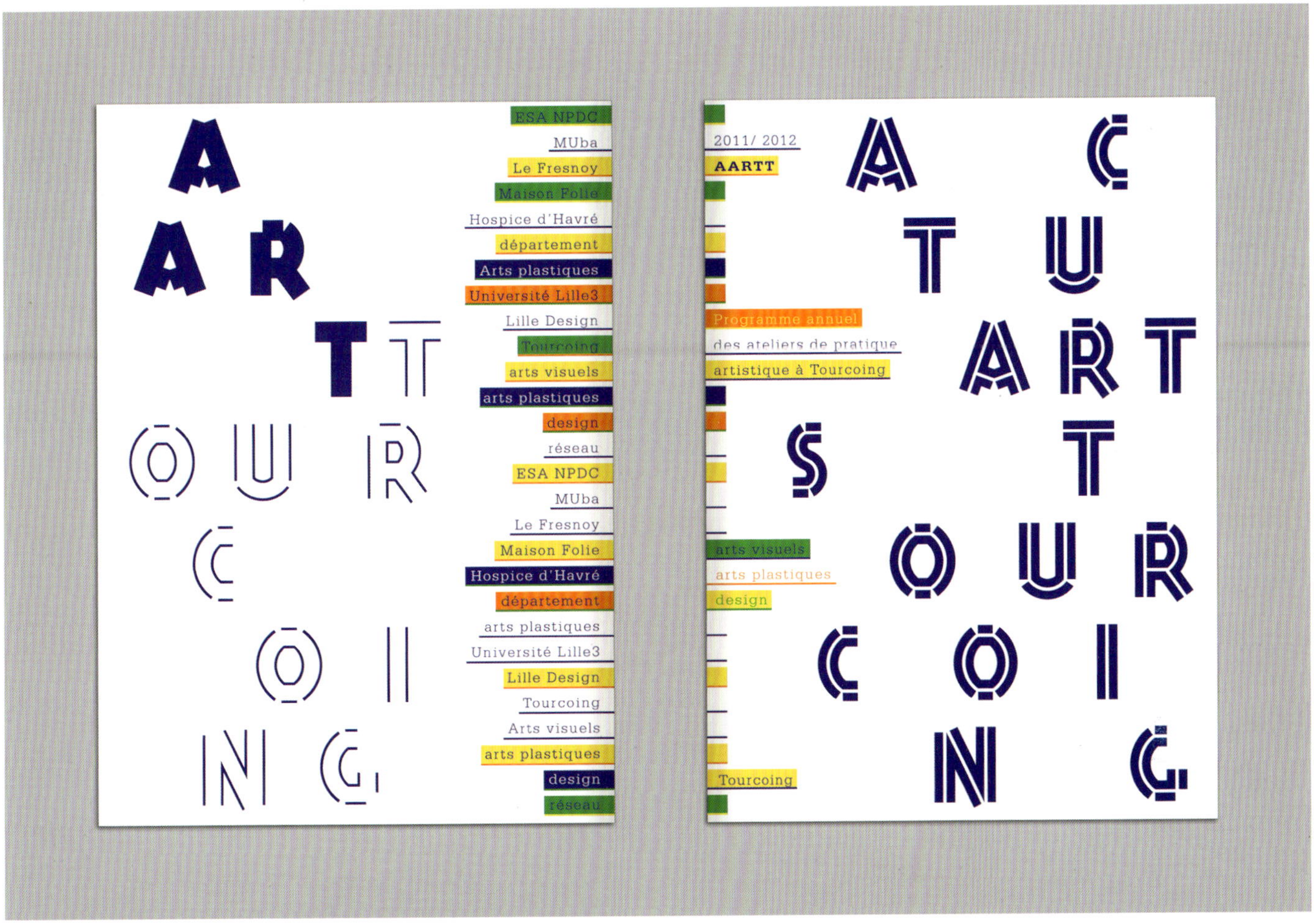

JE SUIS VENUE P 06 VOUS DIRE QU'IL ÉTAIT TEMPS DE PRENDRE
LA PAROLE. SANS REGRETTER P 11 LA EDAD DE ORO, L'ÂGE D'OR ;
SANS POUR AUTANT FAIRE LA RÉVOLUTION, MAIS POUR NE PAS AVOIR
À DIRE ENSUITE J'AI FAILLI. IL FAUDRAIT ALTERNER ENTRE
EYESOPENEYESCLOSED P 10 ET GARDER LES YEUX OUVERTS POUR CHASSER
LES TARTUFFE ET LES P 14 & P 22 BRITANNICUS QUI ENCOMBRENT NOS VIES
À MÉTRAGES VARIABLES. P 12 POUR EXPRIMER NOTRE ADMIRATION POUR
P 32 & 26 LE BLEU VENISE, LES ONCLE VANIA, LES P 16 MARCEL ET SON ORCHESTRE
OU LES P 18 CITÉ BABEL QUI LES ILLUMINENT. PLONGER DANS
PUDIQUE ACIDE/EXTASIS P 40 POUR SE DIRE QUE, COMME À LA MAISON, P 38
UN JOUR J'IRAI À VANCOUVER POUR UN P 68 & 20 COMING OUT SANS AVOIR
PEUR, COMME SISYPHE, P 34 D'ESCALADER LES MONTAGNES ET D'AVOIR
MAL(E). P 24 POUR NE PAS ÊTRE CELUI QUI DIRA PLUS TARD, J'AI FRÉMI. P 54
POUR NE PAS AVOIR PEUR DE CROIRE QUE INDIGENCE=ÉLÉGANCE P 42 ET
GRAPHISME : BENOÎT BODHUIN
QUE LES PLUS GRANDS DÉFILÉS SONT P 28 & P 36 THEM NO GO SEE, CEUX QUE
L'ON NE VOIT PAS. POUR FAIRE TABULARAZA P 30 DE LA LÂCHETÉ ET DE
LA BÊTISE ET ACCEPTER LE P 44 VRAI SPECTACLE, CELUI OÙ L'ON PEUT
P 52 SORTIR DU CORPS POUR ALLER DU CÔTÉ DES EDENCENTRAL, P 60 DES
BLACK'N'BLUES ET P 50 & P 64 DES MÉTAMORPHOSES MAGIC SHOW. POUR
PROFITER DES P 48 - 56 - 59 & 66 POPUP, DES POGO, DES ROMANE, DES DRAGIBUS ET
DES DANSES LIBRES. POUR FAIRE EN SORTE QUE LES SALVES P 58 SOIENT
DES VIVAT ET NOUS RÉCHAUFFENT LE CŒUR. POUR ESPÉRER ENFIN
LE VIVAT - PLACE SAINT VAAST 59280 ARMENTIÈRES - 03 20 77 18 77 - CONTACT@LEVIVAT.NET - WWW.LEVIVAT.NET
QUE LE PARLEMENT, LE VRAI, SOIT CELUI OÙ L'ON PRENNE
LIBREMENT LA PAROLE SUR LE MONDE.

LOVE ! P 62

SAISON 2011-2012

Licence cat.1 120534 • cat.2 120535 • cat.3 120536

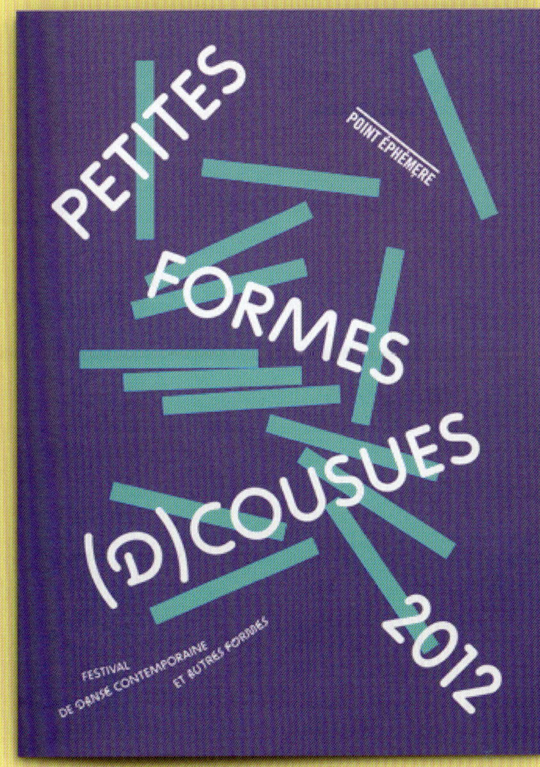

Why is there a trend of combining classical elements with modern design nowadays?

As for graphic design, the general trend is to simplify the drawing. Compared with the extreme grotesque, any typography seems mannered. But more geometrization or extreme simplification of design becomes nearly impossible, so contemporary designers will be interested in more expressive typography and some even tend to express only through typography, which amounts to (re-)sophistication of drawing.

This return to the expressiveness finds probably its source in the movements of the past. There are a myriad of trends besides modernism and classicism, and I think since one decade or two, thanks to the internet that gives access to different cultures, there is a tendency to mix styles and cultures. It is as if we tried to assimilate one century of history of graphic design in one decade. There is another factor that explains this blend: the computer and desktop publishing tools free graphic design from a heavy process industry, which permits designers to release creativity.

How do you achieve an eclectic style with a classic and modern feel in typeface design?

Typography is a work of details. Each type family has these characteristics, just playing with the references of each family to evoke a particular period. For example, neglecting the optical correction will give a very geometric character, or accentuate contrasts strongly referring to Didone, or change the endings (round, rectangular serif...). We can thus play with all the typographical features, modulate the appearance and even be a little irreverent and make styles collide.

How does a font express certain messages or qualities like elegant, edgy, sober, warm or cold, etc.?

These are the fundamentals of design: rhythm, shape, thickness, etc. and also a set of cultural references: elegance may be evoked by Didone for example, and also by the simplicity of a character or the refinement of its design, etc. The warmness can be expressed in curves and volutes (maternal warmth, or arm that embraces you, etc) and so on. It is a combination of the drawing expressiveness and cultural allusions.

Why do some people think serif more of a classic style and sans serif more of a modern style?

It is chronological: serif dates back to the beginning of printing while sans serif dates back to a little over one century and becomes widespread since half century.

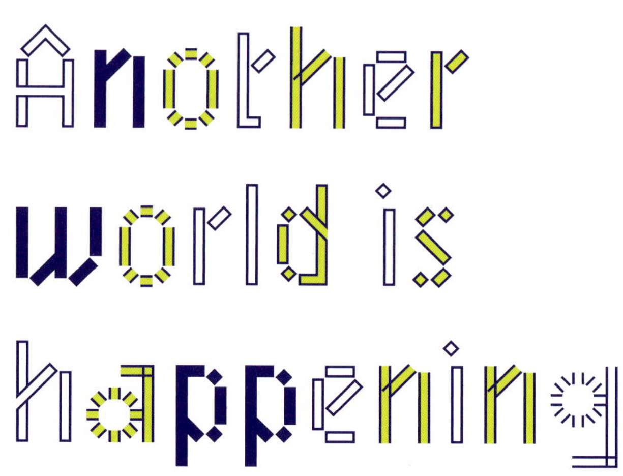

Étape de Scénario décrivant la journée immersive au HUB Bruxelles

HUB gest network password: eatfries

Portes
Ouvertes
9 février 201
de 10h à 18h
École supérieure
d'art de Cambrai
7 rue du Paon
59 400 Cambrai
Tél. 03 27 72 78 78
création
Benoît Bodhuin

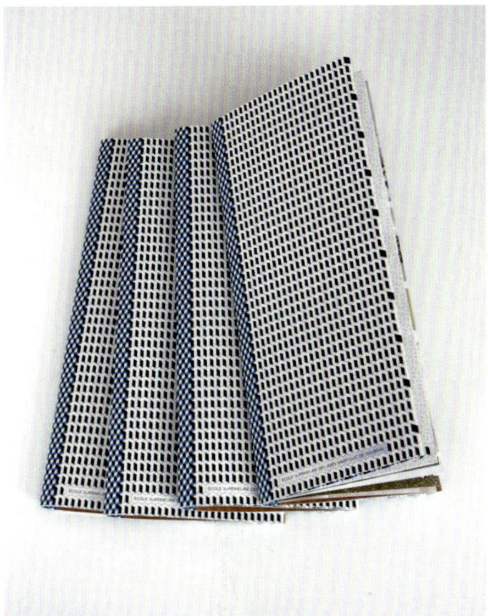

How do you usually choose a typeface in brand design?

First I think we should be clear that typography, like a logo for example, cannot express all personality or traits of a brand. This is to express the main features and to avoid the pitfalls. Then it depends on what this writing is intended for: does it have an emblem function and support the brand identity? Or is it a type to compose the body text of communication documents or to the signage? Once this is determined, it is an expressive play of allusions and inventiveness: the designer plays with the currents and features of the typeface design (period, style, rhythm, form, thickness, etc) and injects all the inventiveness necessary to find the right expression.

INTERVIEW WITH

Zhihong Wang

Chinese Graphic Designer

Zhihong Wang, born in 1975 in Taipei, is a leading graphic designer based in Taiwan and AGI member since 2015. He started his studio in 2000 and has been collaborating with trade publishers in launching his imprints, featuring translated titles on art and design since 2008.

► How did you get into the field of editorial design? Do books have special appeal to you?

I didn't intend to do editorial design. Design projects in publishing industry are not on a large scale and would not bring the designer much money, so it seems that publishing industry isn't as much profit-driven as other fields. I think it is the purity that makes itself different and attracts me most.

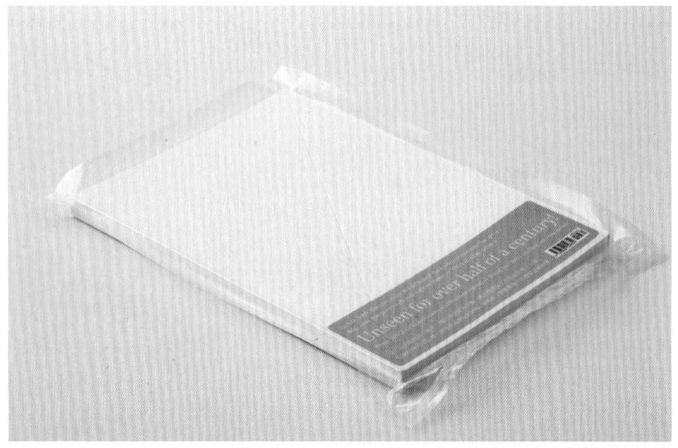

Outside Myself
True Freedom Lies in Subtlety
Deep Cultivation Lies in Joy

時代之眼

You have said, "Cover design is a kind of packaging, but the intention of packaging is not only to reflect the reality (content)." So what are your other pursuits in cover design?

Someone has already done the job of reflecting the reality, so I choose to "create the reality (content)". My designs always run parallel with the content, because I don't think the cover design is wholly dependent on the content or the two elements contradict each other. People who think so may believe that there is only one kind of reality and only one answer to all things.

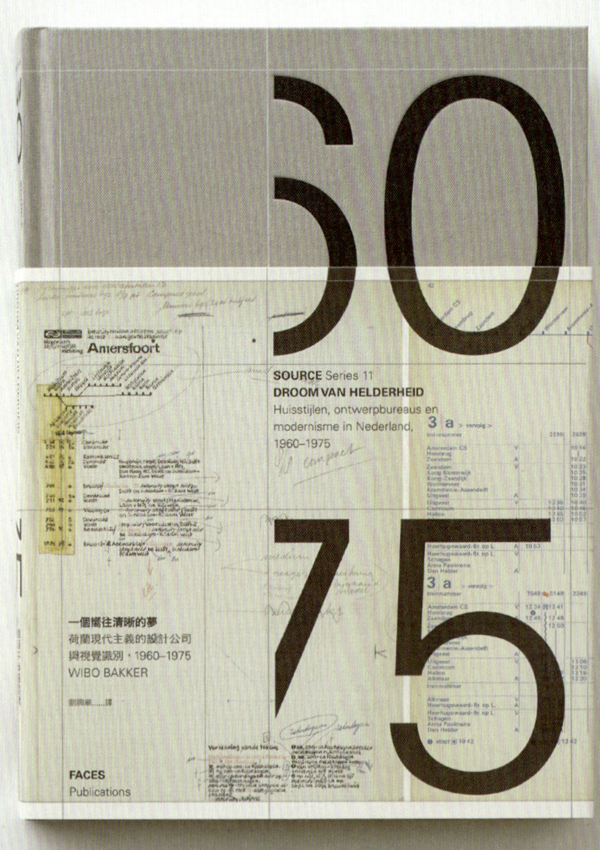
60
75
SOURCE Series 11
DROOM VAN HELDERHEID
Huisstijlen, ontwerpbureaus en modernisme in Nederland, 1960–1975
一個嚮往清晰的夢
荷蘭現代主義的設計公司
與視覺識別，1960–1975
WIBO BAKKER
FACES
Publications

Typography is an important part of editorial design, because text is the key medium of communication as well as design element. What do you take into account when designing Chinese characters?

Maybe the heaviness of a character. Chinese characters generally have many strokes and tend to be square in structure, which may lead to visual bulkiness. Therefore, how to make Chinese characters delicate, graceful and full of individuality is a knowledge.

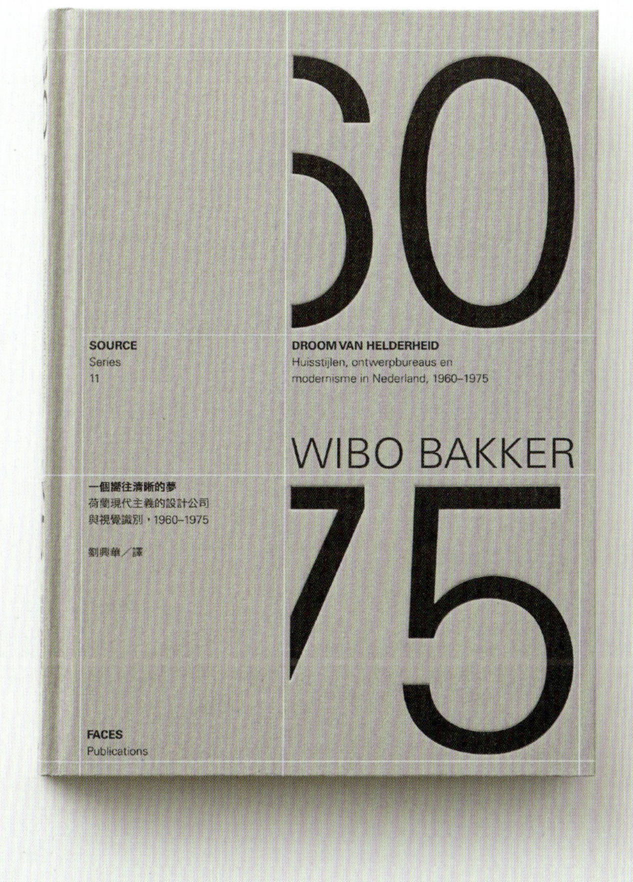

Some argues that text is the focus of editorial design and images are to help convey the information. Do you agree with that? How do you strike a balance between text and visual content in design?

Personally, I seldom use images in my design and text is always my main focus, but I won't underestimate the power of images. Choose text as well as images meticulously and clarify their relationship, and then you can achieve the balance.

Why did you launch the two book series, Source and Insight?

In the past it was the publishing companies that decided which books to publish. I felt designers and readers hardly had the opportunity to read the best and important books of design and art. So I discussed with publishing companies as a designer as well as a reader to forge collaboration. I hope that more and more books would be delicately chosen and produced for the public.

INTERVIEW WITH

Rodrigo Saiani

Typography Designer

Rodrigo Saiani, founder of Plau as well as typeface design instructor at Miami Ad School/ESPM Rio de Janeiro.

► To begin with, I have to admit that I was totally innocent of the fact that there are typeface designers in the world before working on this typography issue. I am sorry for that and that is also my first question: how does it feel being a type designer? What do type designers do actually?

Lol, I guess a lot of people think fonts come out of the blue. Indeed it's quite the opposite – to make fonts people take for granted, a lot of blood, sweat and tears are involved. It's time consuming at best. Just as a drastic example, to make a typeface for Chinese, we're talking about drawing 20.000+ glyphs. I guess it's the work of a lifetime!

That being said, it's a great pleasure. The feeling is a little bit like you're making part of history, by following the footsteps of inventors, artisans, engineers from way back until today. For me it's a rather therapeutic process and I enjoy it quite a bit.

ABCDEFGHIJKLMN
OPQRSTUVWXYZ
abcdefghijklmn
opqrstuvwxyz
0123456789

What sparked your interest in typeface design?

I wasn't very good at drawing faces/bodies, etc., so I ended up doodling letters and when I realized there was a whole universe related to creating letterforms and making them work, I was hooked.

What did you do to get into this brand new universe?

Reading books like crazy. Funny enough, my love for type came when I was attending business school, so I felt both awkward and unprepared to design my own fonts. So I studied, participated in forums, eventually attended a workshop or two and looked through the work of everyone I knew at the time (Neville Brody, Erik Spiekermann, Adrian Frutiger were instrumental in my education). It was only when I started doing it that all that reading started taking shape.

There are five fonts displayed in Plau's website: three sans-serifs and two serifs. Does that mean you have a preference for sans? Why do you start designing the serifs?

Just a quick correction: there are 3 sans, 1 serif (Tenez) and 1 script (Primot). I'd say there's a natural inclination towards sans-serifs. When I saw Frutiger (the typeface) for the first time, I marveled at the simple, humane shapes, and that inspired me to design my own interpretation of the perfect sans (a sort of holy grail every designer pursues eventually). It took a long time until I realized I should try out some calligraphy to learn from where type design came from. That leads me into trying out scripts and seriffed designs for a change. The reason is simple: to learn a new approach and solidify that learning into a product. My intention is to be as versatile as possible and to be able to tackle a wide range of styles.

By the way, Google has just released its new logo which is a sans-serif. What do you think of it?

I can't really tell what the process was, but in my opinion it's a missed opportunity. I really like what they did in animation and icons, but the logotype itself could have been more expressive. Every company seems to be making the geometric sans move these days, and it feels a little lazy and may show a lack of typographic dare. It's getting easier to differentiate any brand these days: just don't make it Upper/Lowercase geometric sans-serifs and you got it.

Is Tenez your latest work? How does it come out and would you recommend something like how and where to use it?

Yes, Tenez is our first venture into serif type design. We were really interested in flexible nib calligraphy (the kind which inspired fonts like Bodoni, Didot and the such) and decided it was time to try it out and also explore organic and non simplified shapes, which is much harder to design and manage.

Plus, we had a project for a shoe company branding which would really benefit from that aesthetic. In the end, we're really proud of how it came together (we're working on the italics at the time of this interview).

Tenez is a display typeface, meant to be used in fairly large sizes. My dream application would be for tennis related projects. I'm a big fan and the font name - Tenez - is inspired by the French word which titled the sport. But the best thing is when designers grab what we've done and use it in unexpected ways, so I really hope to see some cool applications popping up soon.

Some argues a type should not be expressive; it should be neutral to display the information. From the opposite, some believes a type is individual enough to convey a certain mood. What is your opinion?

It definitely depends on context. There will always be situations in which the typeface must hide and make room for the content and others when the typeface IS the message.

I started my journey believing strongly in the Crystal Goblet thing. Nowadays I find myself trying harder and harder to make typefaces that are expressive. There's always room for both. The important thing to learn is when, where and how to use these tools to honour the message – be it making an impact or humbly standing away from it.

How about the role of typography in branding?

I like Spiekermann's quote that a typeface IS a brand. It creates connection and recognizability right away, especially when messages are repeated time and again such as in the case of brand communication. I'd like to compare the typeface/typography to the brand's stem cells, for it can be shaped into any message and form the brand wishes to convey. That's how important an asset I think great type is to any company that wants to make a positive impact in the world.

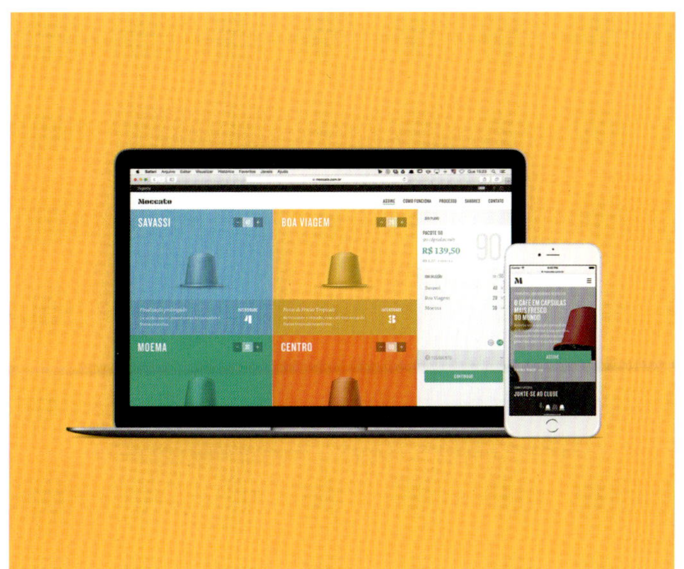

What typeface do you frequently use in your own daily life? Would you use merely one or two or change it frequently?

Our studio uses our own Guanabara Sans as the corporate typeface so I see it every day. I find myself testing Neutraface 2 by House Industries all the time, just never let me down. Dolly by Underware is by far my favorite book face. I try to use typefaces that match the particularities of the brief and be open to trying out new stuff. I don't consider myself a talented type matcher, maybe this is why I decided to start designing my own.

Being a Rio de Janeiro based designer, what typeface do you think can be a typeface for the city?

We tried to answer that very question with Guanabara Sans so I think it's that one (laughs)! It's definitely a very difficult task to take the personality of a city and create a typeface out of it. The challenge is to make it subtle and legible while giving it enough personality so that when people are told that's the city's font they go: Ah! I see... I don't really think one would be able to tell that's Rio typeface straight away unless you used very cliché forms from the city.

In our case, the limitation was it needed to be good for signage and other informational texts. That leads to certain shapes and forms that probably wouldn't happen otherwise.

Dalton Maag did a great job with the Olympic typeface. They actually took the landscape and hints, and turned it into a functional and expressive display typeface so I guess we have a good pairing there: Titles + Text.

Is there any type designer or typographer you like?

I have a special thing for Frutiger (Univers, Frutiger and Meridien being long time favorites), but there are so many others worth knowing. So I'll take this question and use it to talk about my Brazilian friends who are doing amazing work today: Daniel Sabino from Blackletra, Eduílson Coan from Dootype, Marconi Lima from Typefolio, Just in Type and so many others. The Brazilian type scene is blossoming and very much worth a deeper look.

INTERVIEW WITH

Aaron Nieh

Chinese Typography Designer

Aaron Nieh is one of the leading graphic designers in Taiwan and founder of Aaron Nieh Workshop. Widely known for his album package and publication design, Aaron is an award-winning designer; some of the awards include Best Album Package Design of Golden Melody(2010, 2014 and 2015) in Taiwan, Red Dot Communication Design Award and IF Communication Design in Germany. He was one of the jurors of the 2013 Red Dot Communication Design Award, and now he is a resident of 18th Street Arts Center and an AGI member.

▶ In most of your works, typefaces of book titles are specially designed, how do you mix your design concept with the choice of typefaces?

I'll just follow my heart and try to imagine what the typefaces should look like. In fact, not all the book titles would require design on the characters. We don't need to design types if the book title already comes with a beautiful meaning.

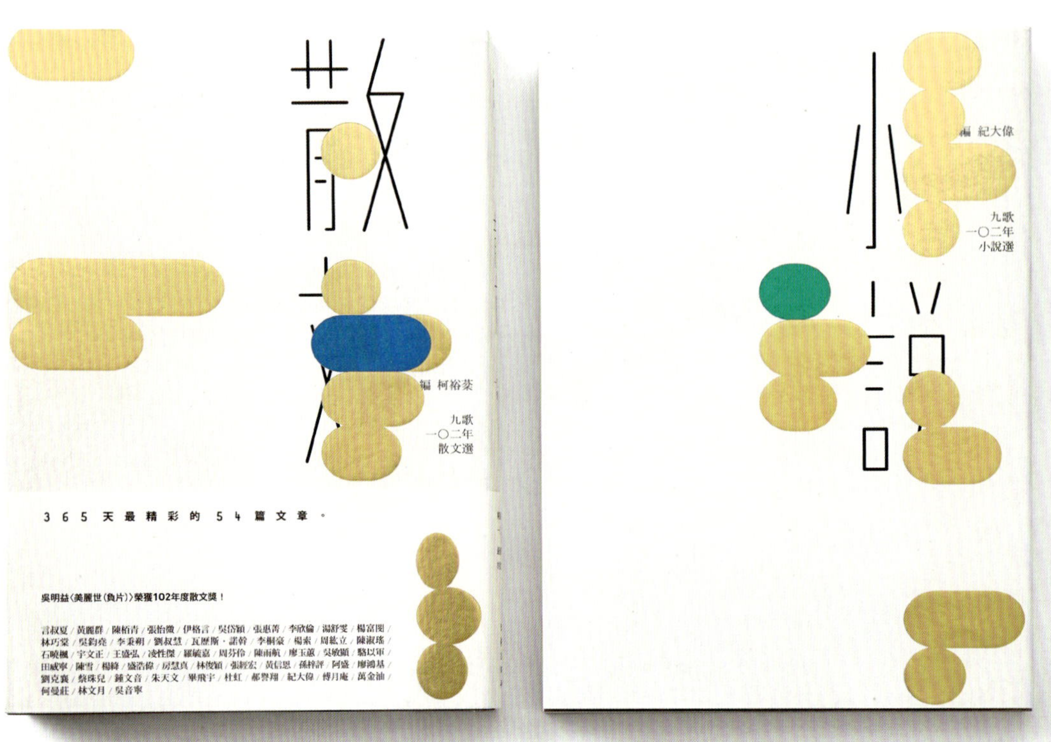

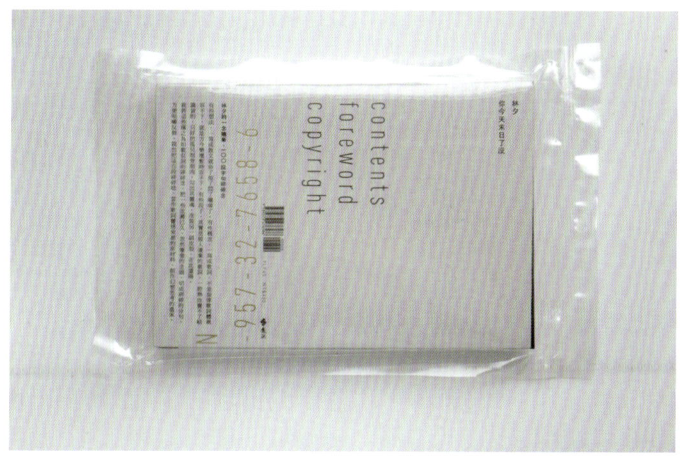

Book cover gives the first impression of a book; it can either indicate or hide the content. Take Albert Leung's book 你今天末日了沒 (meaning:did you live like you're dying today)as an example, what are your design beliefs?

For designers, finding images from a book title or content could be challenging. The book gives a sense of sadness, but as far as I see it, the writer's Chinese name 林夕 and 末日 (meaning: end of the world, dying)can be lovely and special through changes of the typeface Heiti. By making the cover a little more delightful, all coldness, death and ends are softened. That's why the book doesn't look scary even with a ghost on the cover. When people look at the book and find it cute, they'll feel relieved about death and the end of the world.

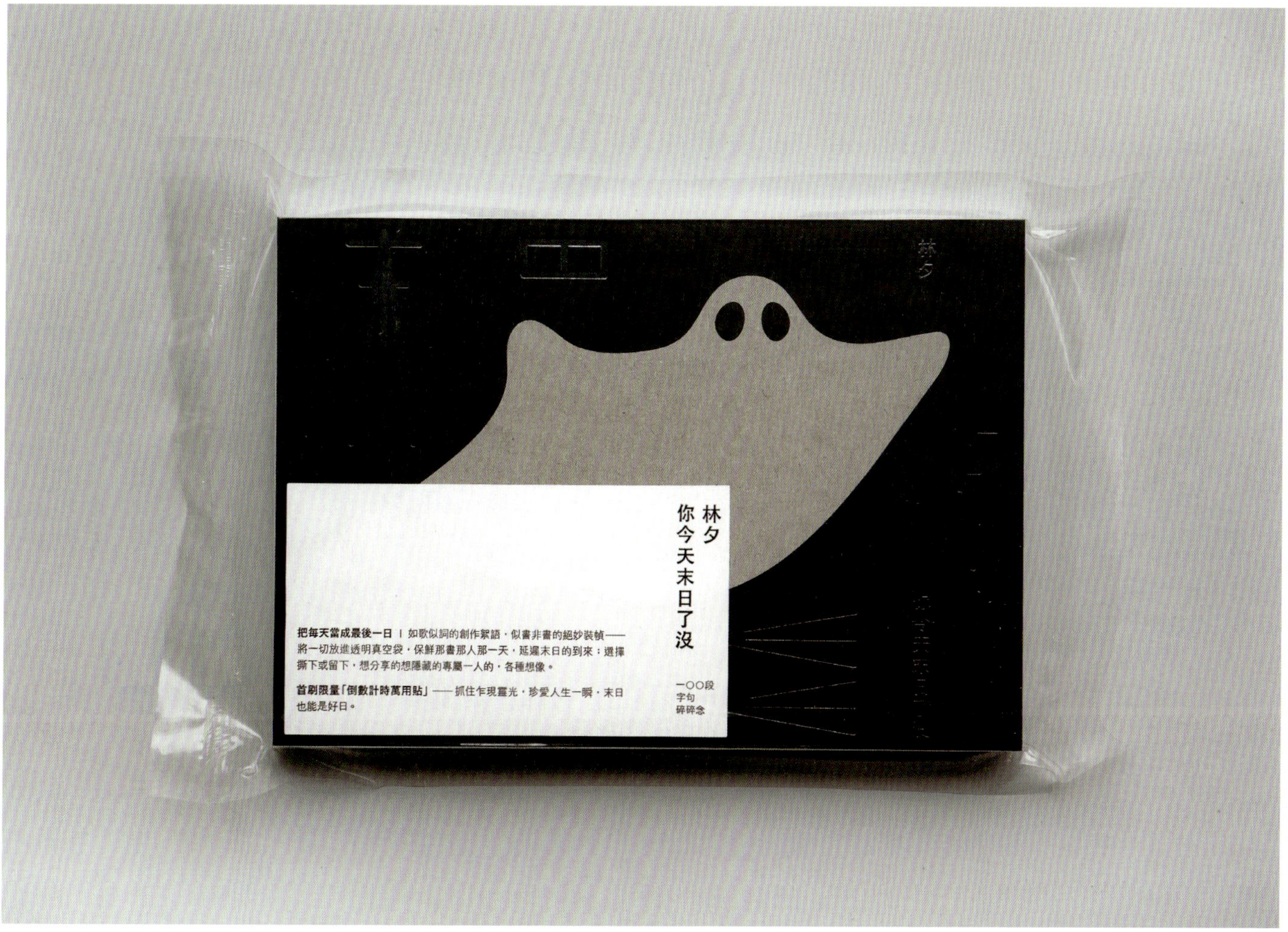

From inside out, the body text and design of a book must blend perfectly, and they should flatter each other. Where do you usually start when designing a project?

If we're designing the whole book, we'll usually finish the inner pages first, then the binding and layout, and cover. I believe that it is best to end the whole design with the cover, because it is most accurate for unifying the whole style of the book.

Typefaces and layout used in body texts could affect one's reading experience. What would you take into consideration when working on typefaces and layout in body text?

I'll usually follow my instinct and use the typeface Song or Heiti. Typefaces should never stand out while displayed in content, otherwise readers might be distracted. This is what I try to balance.
About layouts, I would usually arrange certain blank spaces, which can make the page a bit more prose-like and graceful. These empty spaces will also make it more comfortable and breathable for the readers, which I think is necessary.

Are there any typefaces that you prefer to use in body text?

Yes. There are some type foundries that produce typefaces specially-designed for body texts; they are universal design fonts that are more legible and readable. I prefer them because they're more enjoyable for long-time reading.

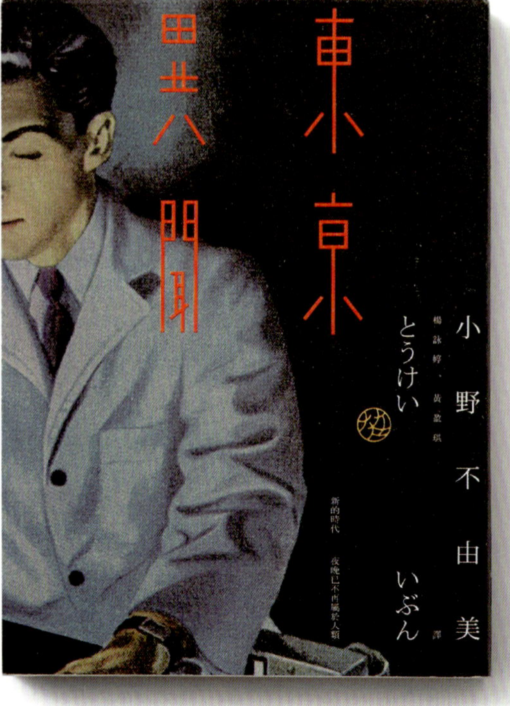

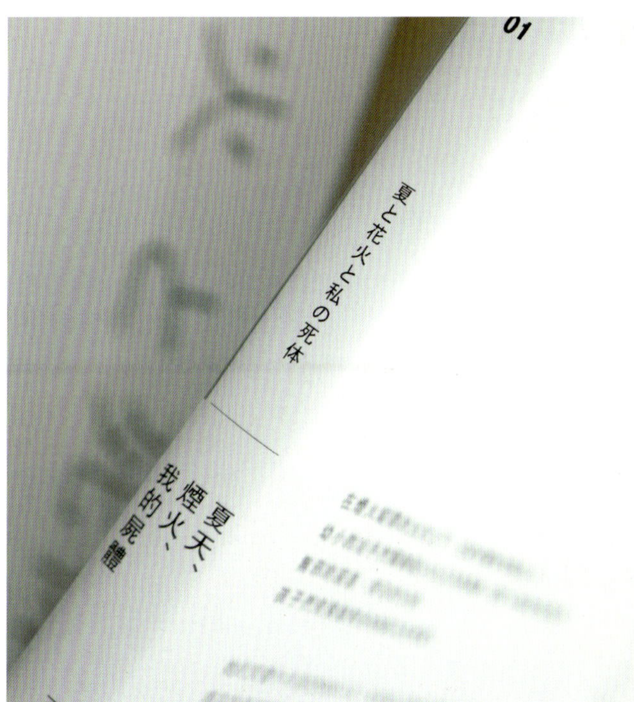

You designed books for clients from mainland China and your own book is also available in simplified Chinese. So in your opinion, what are the differences between simplified and traditional Chinese?

A lot of people think that traditional Chinese looks better on books. But I believe that there is no such thing as good or bad typefaces; there're only right or wrong ones.

Designs that are overdone may not provide good reading experience, and you've mentioned that the best designs are the ones that are adequate and not-disturbing. How do you achieve this adequateness, especially in terms of reading experience?

I don't like info-bombing, and I never feel worried if my design is simple. Usually I'll stop at the moment when the idea is neatly expressed. Then I won't try to add any visual elements. It is only right to leave for the readers to interpret the design.

Do you have any criteria while choosing projects to work on? Would you offer to design for writers or contents you like?

I'll usually listen to my heart during inquiry, because you can do it well only if you like it. Usually I won't try to fight for a design, or try to get involved with editors' decisions. I don't have to do all the designs. There're many great designers who do very great book designs, and I enjoy their works.

INTERVIEW WITH

Panos Vassiliou

Designer of DIN TEXT PRO & Regal Pro

DIN TEXT PRO

In 1936 the German Standards Committee Deutsches Institut für Normung(DIN) officially proposed DIN 1451 as the standard type of lettering to be used in the field of road traffic. The purpose of this standard was to lay down a style of lettering which is timeless and easily legible. Unfortunately, these early letters lacked elegance and were not properly designed for typographic applications.

Ever since, several type foundries adopted the original designs for digital photocomposition. The first digital versions were released in 1990 by Adobe but only in four basic variations. Similar ones were also released by URW.

By early 2000, it became apparent that the existing DIN-based fonts did not fulfil the ever-increasing demand of complex corporate projects for more weights and support for additional languages.

Parachute® was set out to fill this gap by introducing the DIN Text series which, ever since, has become the most comprehensive and sophisticated set of DIN typefaces ever. It was based on the original standards but was specifically designed to fit typographic requirements. Completed in 2002, it was first released in 2003 with support for Latin and Greek.

By 2005, all families were upgraded to include 14 weights,opentype features (small caps, etc.) and extended support for all European languages including Cyrillic. Later, an additional Hairline weight was added to all families. Finally, in 2010 Parachute® released 4 new families DIN Monospace, DIN Stencil, DIN Text Arabic and DIN Text Universal. Altogether the Parachute DIN series is a set of 8 super families with a total of 96 weights.

TYPEWRITERS
context and discourse in terms of contemporary linguostylistics
a day for remembering
The flat-roofed house is distinguished by expanses of first floor glazing
BIOGRAPHY
internet and television dramatically increased international communication
elegant exercise in sculptural massing
brand new provocative covers for the fall fashion issue of the famous woman magazine
modern house style
homogenizing factors are limited due to strong nationalistic forces
GLOCKENSPIEL
context in terms of contemporary linguostylistics

CONTAINED HOUSE
as iron is eaten away by rust, so the envious are consumed by their own passion
SUPREME BEINGS OF LEISURE
The flat-roofed house is distinguished by expanses of first floor glazing
microwave
brand new provocative magazine covers for the summer fashion issue
a perfect day for a walk
internet dramatically increased communication
DESIGN
quiting smoking now reduces risks to your health
sculptural massing
a poetic scene captured on film last december in paris

WORDPRESS MAGAZINE
monthly guide to the best independent record releases
oldstyle typewriters
analyzing the complex structure of biomolecules
HOMEWORK
Analyzing macromolecular structures with native mass spectrometry
Massage revitalization
gendered innovations in science and engineering
meaningful
an elegant exercise in sculptural massing
Main Fashion Floor
technology is the campfire around which we tell our stories
WINTERBOARD
the computer is a mindless speed machine
home decoration

MAIN FASHION FLOOR

un shopping abordable et de qualité pour fashionistas en quête d'exotisme

SUPREME BEINGS OF LEISURE

this house is a happy blend of high tech and traditional elements

RELEASED

MOREOVER, TELEVISION DRAMATICALLY INCREASED INTERNATIONAL COMMUNICATION

MODERN DECORATION

simple minimal design that delivers function

CHANGE

the Information Technology Marketplace will boost global cultures

not tested on animals

Peacekeepers observe peace processes in conflict areas

EXPERIMENTATION

mass market graphic activism in progress

▶ How was the Din Text Pro developed from the original version?

I used the original design published by the German Standards Committee which includes the basic letterforms in one rather unclear version. Some of these letters were scanned to give me a rough background sketch. Based on this, I started designing a few basic glyphs which I always design first such as "a", "n", "o" and "g". Everything else was designed based on these letterforms and a visual reference to the original. The regular weight was completed and using that as a base I designed all other weights and variations.

What are the typographic requirements for redesigning this typeface? What is the intention of redesigning it?

The original DIN was designed by engineers with a rather mechanical construction. The purpose of the redesign was to make the appropriate optical corrections which are essential when you design a typeface. For example, in mono linear typefaces like DIN, the horizontal lines must be lighter than the vertical lines; the middle bar of letter "E" must be placed a bit higher in order to look as if it sits in the middle; the upper and lower part of letter "O" must be lighter than the rest in order for its weight to look even and so on.

What are the main applications of the fonts with different weights?

Mostly print applications like magazines and newspapers use many variations. Aside from that, single weights may be useful in different applications. For instance, a hairline weight may find its place in a fashion Ad.

What do you think are the latest trends for typeface design industry in the digital age?

I think it would be typeface super families which support many different scripts.

REGAL PRO

The objective of this project was to design a typeface for Grazia magazine. It was later revamped and redesigned for other commercial use. According to the brief, this typeface had to be elegant, luxurious, sexy and vibrant, to reflect the female sensitivity and take into consideration the modern woman. Targeting this consumption-wise and well-educated woman, a typeface that is not strictly based on classical forms, but incorporates several distinct elements that express the personality of a modern woman and the products she consumes is repaired. For that matter, elegant curvy details were introduced in order to create a link to the female figure; teardrop terminals which reflect a woman's sensitivity; pronounced quirks on upper and lower arms for her eyelashes; high-contrast, sharp corners at thinning terminals for her high heels; alternate glyphs for the woman who prefers to express her individuality by using various accessories which can dramatically change her appearance; elegant endings and long curves to reflect her predisposition to dream; bell-shaped serifs with an inward rather than outward direction which recall streamlined seventies fashion. This series of typefaces is diverse in its construction as it consists of five related super families i.e. text, display, finesse, swash and stencil. These families share common attributes but they differ in content according to each one's usage.

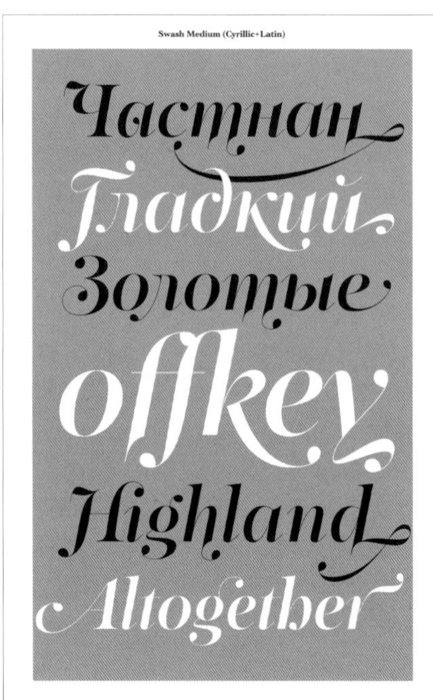

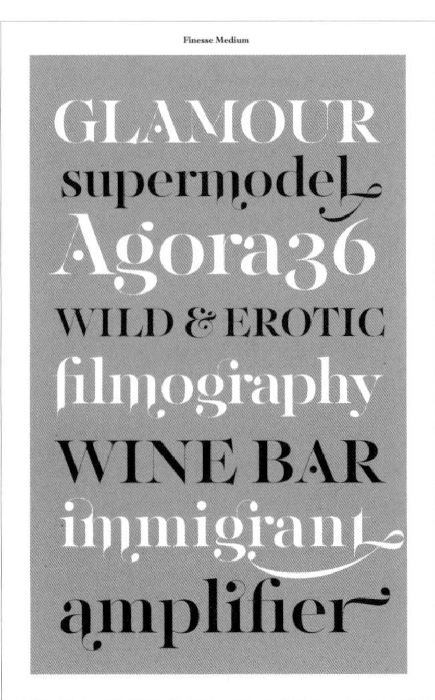

▶ Except magazines, do you think Regal also works well on user interface?

Designers would select low-contrast fonts for interfaces basically because common mobiles and computer screens limit the performance of high-contrast fonts. The new Retina displays though, have high enough density to restrict pixelation which allows high-contrast fonts to display well on these devices. Despite that, I have seen Regal being used successfully on web and iPad apps such as by S Moda, the Spanish fashion magazine.

Various Distinct Letterforms

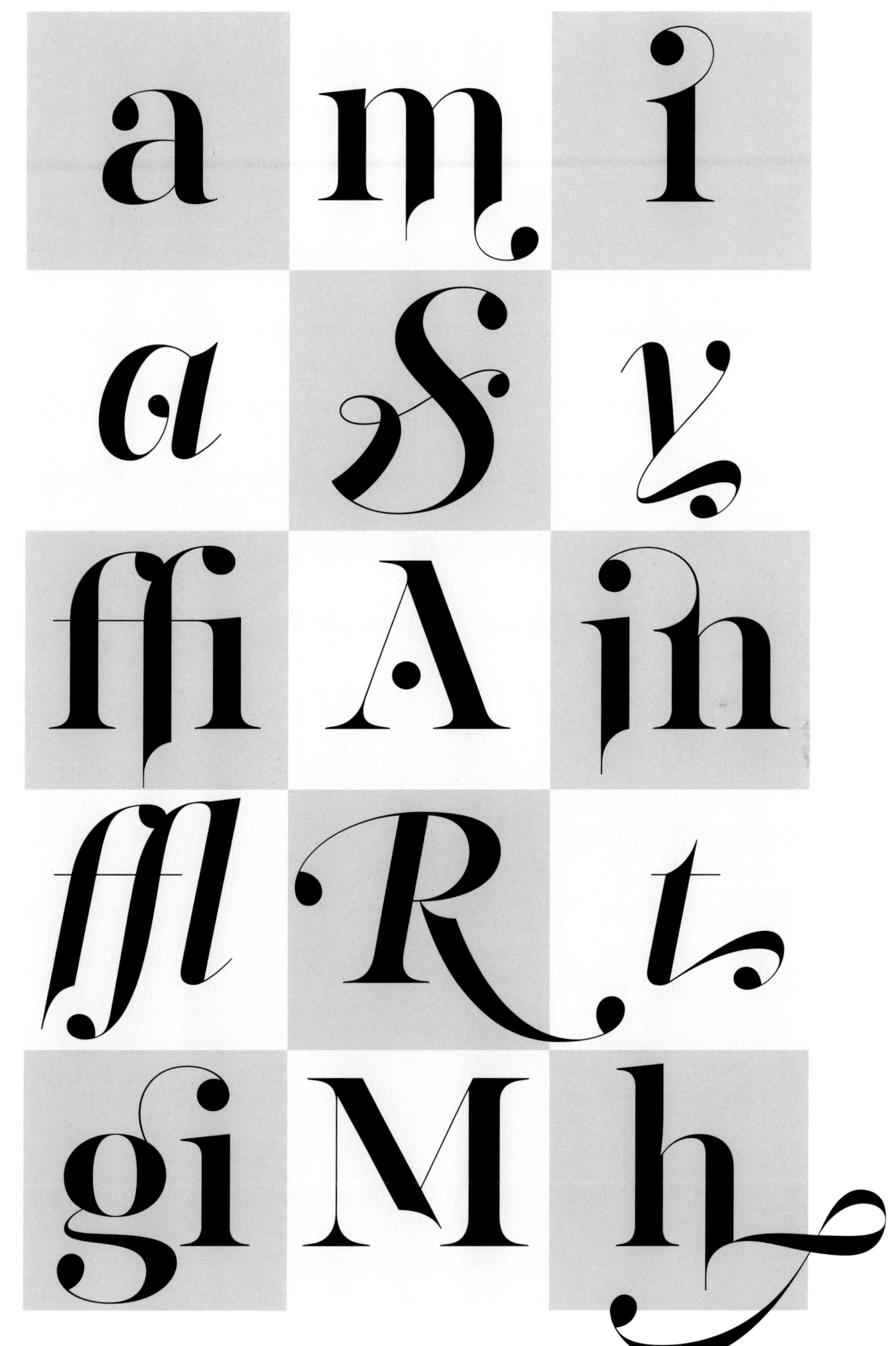

Display Version

Wohlstand

Hollywood is banking that they will be next year's new dynamic duo

provocative magazine covers

a unique symphony for piano and orchestra

monumental marble staircase, a glossy paean to the hard-edged cool

instrumentalism

the best of the european runways

COCKTAIL RECIPES

this house is a happy blend of high tech and traditional elements

amplifier

an elegant exercise in sculptural massing

music performance

collaborating with some of the sharpest creative minds

imagination

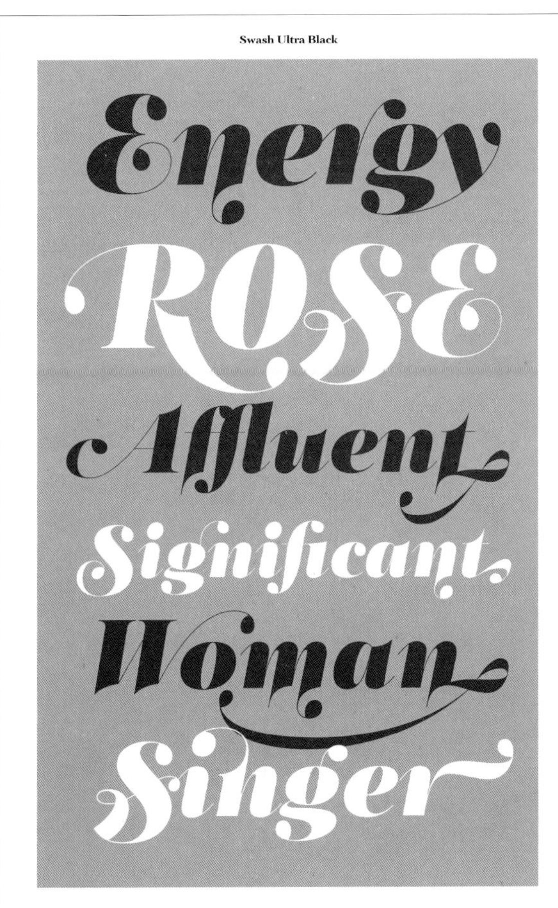

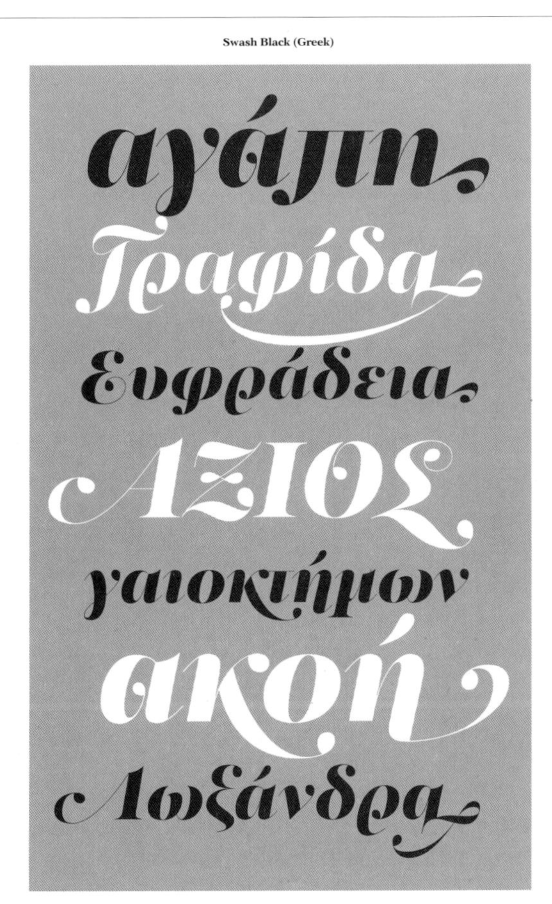

What do you think of PF Regal Text Pro as a robust forward-thinking serif typeface?

This version of Regal is intended mainly for body text and as such it was designed to have a balanced contrast, a clean look, large x-height and be legible at small sizes. Furthermore, it incorporates certain attributes such as the bell-shaped serifs which set it apart from similar-minded typefaces.

What are the characteristics of other typefaces that match PF Regal Pro?

Regal has a distinct personality, so I would use it next to a quiet grotesque sans serif typeface such as Helvetica, a geometric typeface such as Futura, or a legible contemporary sans such as PF Centro Sans Pro.

How did you balance beauty and legibility of PF Regal Pro?

Well, you really have to do your math, and you have to do a lot of research in order to understand your subject before you start a new project. The Regal project was really demanding in that sense, so I started by putting together the functional aspects (readability/legibility) first i.e. the Regal Text typeface and then moved ahead to create a more elegant version and embellish it with beautiful high-contrasting or swashy parts such as in Regal Finesse.

What do you think are the hottest trends of typeface design?

I think high-contrast serif as well as low-contrast mono-linear sans serif fonts and classical designs of the past with a contemporary twist are popular now.

Typography in Data Visualization

Typography matters more than what we think in data visualization. It is not only an approach to express what the story is about, but also an intuitive and subtle access that allows readers to capture the style and the theme of the info-graphic as quickly as possible. In diverse contents, the selection of typography serves multiple intentions; some value functionality while others appreciate beauty.

Yet in most cases, functionality and beauty are intertwined and hard to be balanced. Another major challenge for data visualization, just like the everlasting issue in the design world, would lie in how designers use visual languages to create an appropriate info-graphic based on their inspirations and the requirements from the client, sequentially meeting the needs and expectations of readers. Typography, under these circumstances, shares the burden.

In addition, due to the rapid growth of typeface design and enhancement of data visualization design tools, massive possibilities of typography have been introduced to data visualization design. In an age when data visualization has been considered as a combination of multidisciplinary subjects, we are all curious about how essential typography is in it.

Therefore, we interviewed Sven Ehmann, Creative Director of Gestalten, to pick his brains about how typography works in data visualization.

INTERVIEW WITH

Sven Ehmann

Creative Director of Gestalten, specializing in developing visual concepts and contents across all media

What do you think of the saying that data visualization is the combination of science, art and design?

To me, data visualization is a visual language with its own grammar, which is developed at the intersection of journalism, design and software development. It can be used to report about each and every subject and hopefully finds the ones that are interesting and relevant enough so that we as the readers will understand our world today better than before. Since data visualization is a form of storytelling, it is not meant to just create an editorial atmosphere; it needs to be communicated in a straightforward manner on all levels.

Are there any special features of typefaces used in data visualization?

The single most important requirement for typefaces used in data visualization should be readability. Since space is almost always a crucial issue in data visuals, typefaces that are compact but still highly readable – even in rather small font sizes–are used the most. Therefore, typefaces that offer a condensed version are favorable. Another key factor for choosing a typeface is the output medium. For those working in print only, the criteria will be different from that for others who work in digital as well.

EX
EW
CR
EN
VU
ENDANGERED
RED LIST
0.5
AMAZONA
FESTIVA
KINGDOM: ANIMALIA
PHYLUM: CHORDATA
CLASS: AVES
ORDER: PSITTACIFORMES
SUPERFAMILY: PSITTACOIDEA
FAMILY: PSITTACIDAE
SUBFAMILY: ARINAE
TRIBE: ANDROGLOSSINI
GENUS: AMAZONA
SPECIES: A. FESTIVA
SUM | SPR | WIN | FAL
ANIMALIA
CHORDATA
AVES
PSITTACIFORMES
PSITTACOIDEA
PSITTACIDAE
GEOGRAPHIC RANGE:
INFO

How do typefaces contribute to the readability in data visualization?

Typefaces introduce a clear structure and hierarchy of information, which will help the readers navigate even complex visualizations. They can set different content levels apart from one to another and also separate them from more functional elements, like texts for orientation, keys or instructions. The higher the complexity or level of a visual's abstraction, the more important it is to clearly indicate to the readers where to start and where to go from there. The Italian information design studio Accurat has developed their very nice and reader-friendly habit of not just providing keys for their graphics but also the step-by-step "how to read this" instructions.

What do you think about beauty and functionality are balanced in typography?

I think there is no beauty in typography without functionality, but the function is not necessarily only limited to being a very clear, clean, technical transportation of information. For example, even if text elements in a data visual are realized in a more expressive, hand-drawn illustrational style, it can and should still serve the purpose of narration. It might very well make sense to use a more classic typeface for all basic information, but adding another typeface with a more individual character will catch the readers' attention and guide them through the story or to express the content more appropriately.

Should human-oriented design concept be applied in typography in data visualization?

Absolutely. The production of well-researched and well-executed data visualization takes a lot of time, energy and money. If you as an editor or designer made the decision to invest those resources, you would also want to make sure you reach your audience. That audience should define the specifics of your human- (or maybe rather user-) centered approach. In some cases, your audience might simply be anybody, so the visuals you produce need to be very accessible, even popular. In other cases, you might work for a much defined group of professionals, and then you can shape your visual language to serve their specific interests and knowledge. But the reader is always a key criterion for the design process.

Can typefaces imply the hidden values of the data? How are they related?

Typefaces are mostly used to extend and explain the visual representations of data, but they can also be used to express the data directly, e.g. through their font size or the relation between different font sizes. The key question a designer has to answer before using type to visualize information is whether the graphic will become easier or more difficult to access to the readers. For example, if the difference is too small or too large, the audience will have difficulties in really understanding it. When the precise numbers are important, translation of number might be too much of an abstraction. Any elements matter, so the designer should choose carefully.

How does the typography reflect the concept or the theme of the infographics?

The choice for a particular typeface and its application in an infographic can depend as much on the individual content, as on the editorial context. Some media outlets choose to work with a very limited range of typefaces across all their graphics so that readers feel at home and are not distracted from the content. The New York Times would be a prime example for that. Other media outlets use more expressive typefaces and even turn the text into integral parts of the visuals to attract and even entertain their readers. The Italian magazine IL–a supplement to the daily Il Sole Di 24 Ore–does that in a very playful and highly aesthetic way. There is an ongoing discussion among designers and editors in the field about the right and wrong of what some call an "eye candy" or as Edward Tufte put it, a "chart junk". But maybe that discussion has moved onto being more about "how much" vs. "how little" and the honest interest in developing this language forward is present all around.

What are the current challenges of data visualization design?

Even though data visualization exists for a long time, it has recently reached certain popularity and has seemed to really become an additional universal visual language. What it needs to cope with are a couple of rather different challenges. Inside the discipline, a pressing aspect is to find enough talents to develop the tools and the visual vocabulary further. There is a massive potential since so much data is available now; boiling it down and selecting the important one from the rest is as essential as translating the data into an appropriate visual. Outside the discipline, the challenge is to not just do whatever is possible, but to do what the readers will understand and appreciate as well. The level of visual literacy among a wider public will rise slower than most innovative storytellers would like it to. But on the other hand, it is up to them to raise the bar step by step. Their audiences will be happy to follow, but also be clear when it is too much.

Is there any approach for typography in different content classifications?

There are various options to classify content by the use of typography: different categories can be defined by different typefaces, type sizes, colours and so on, but which way to go depends on the content and the style of visualization. In a very colourful graphic, the typography might rather not use a large number of additional colours while a black and white graphic might work better, if the text is highlighted. A designer needs to understand the different parameters on offering and using them wisely. It also makes a lot of sense to stick with the same logic throughout a story, an issue of a publication or over a period of time so that the readers are not confused by the inconsistency.

What are the requirements for a competent data visualization designer?

A well-trained data visualization designer should know his design tools very well and also understand well enough about the basics of journalism and software development to have constructive conversations with the other people in the team. In rare cases, all three aspects might come together in one single person, but since data visuals are rather complex to produce, it will mostly be a team effort. Beyond that and probably even more important in the long run, there will be another driving force that allows you to stay on top of developments – both in terms of content and tools – and that driving force will always be curiosity.

FROM SCRIPT TO TYPE

"Where can I get a font of the script used in the ITC™ logo?"

Over the years, this has been one of the most consistently asked questions of ITC. The answer was always the same: "You can't. The ITC script logo is hand-lettering and it is not available in a font." At one point, ITC had asked Ed Benguiat, who drew the original logo, to consider enlarging the few characters into a complete typeface, but lack of time to take on such a major project, and the technology to do justice to the design, precluded the task – until now. With the blessings of Benguiat, and taking full advantage of the OpenType™ font format, Jim Wasco, senior designer at Monotype, developed the Elegy™ typeface, a design that captures the grace, verve and remarkable spirit of the original ITC logo.

The working name for the typeface during the early stages of the project was "ITC Script", as shown in Figure 1, but this was changed to "Elegy" as the design neared completion. The reason for the change is that we wanted to give homage to Aaron Burns, one of the original founders of ITC and the company's heart and soul during its formative years. The typeface is our elegy to the man and his contributions. The first line on Figure 1 is the ITC logo and the middle line is an early version of the font Elegy. Note the differences from the logo, like the lowercase "f" loop being less wild. On the bottom is the final Elegy design. Things needed to be changed, and tamer for the design to work as a typeface.

International Typeface Corporation

ITC Logo by Ed Benguiat and Tom Carnase 1970

International Typeface Corporation

Early ITC Script by Jim Wasco 2008

International Typeface Corporation

Final Elegy by Jim Wasco 2010

Figure1 ITC logo compared to ITC Script first draft and Elegy

VALUABLE REFERENCES FROM SCRIPTS

Figure 2 presents a Spencerian script spring steel pen work by Wasco. Copperplate calligraphy, a formal script style of lettering, was developed in the 1700's England used for mercantile, insurance, social and court writing. It was difficult to forge making it a good choice for formal documents. Master engravers and calligraphers produced copybooks to be used as models. Born in America in 1800s, Pratt Rogers Spencer was a penmanship teacher who developed a system for writing like this known as Spencerian script. Samples of this kind of writing were invaluable references for the Elegy typeface.

Figure 2 Piano recital invitation hand lettering sample

It was samples like these shown in Figure 4, hand lettering from the 1700s and 1800s, that were the most useful. The Ames book of Penmanship above was a valuable resource. Many shapes were borrowed from these models.

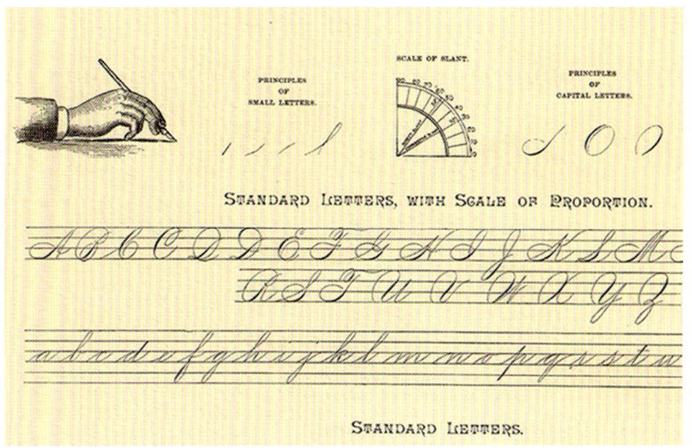

Figure 4 Page from Ames Book of Penmanship

Scripts shown in Figure 3 are other fonts based on copperplate calligraphy. These were, however, not very useful references for Elegy, since it is based heavily on hand lettering.

The quick brown fox

Edwardian Script

The quick brown fox

Bickham Script

Figure 3 Edwardian Script and Bickham Script

Figure 5 is a photograph of copperplate calligraphy. Notice the "Th" ligature. This type of functionality was possible to build into Elegy through OpenType features.

Figure 5 Photo of someone lettering copperplate calligraphy

Figures, punctuation, accents and modern symbols like the sample in Figure 6 were hard to find references for, so they had to be made from scratch. The formal script style of hand lettering from the 1700's was an influence on Bodoni. This is why Neo Classical and Transitional Roman typeface designs are an excellent complement to a script like Elegy. The two styles complement each other. Other shapes in the font, such as the math symbols, were based on some script shapes, a Transitional Roman character, or an extremely thin sans serif typeface.

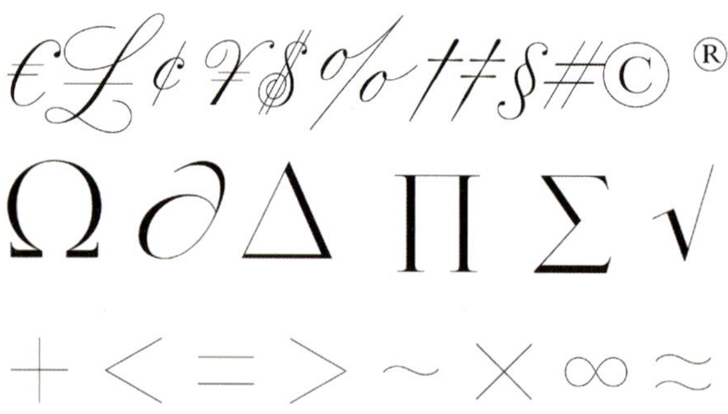

Figure 6 Sample of punctuation and symbols

Handwriting in Figure 7 is mid 1800's manual from Boston. Note two different "f" designs. Also, the letters at the beginnings and ends of words have longer tails, or initial and final forms. This shows how words have initial and final letterforms that are different than the medial forms, similar to the Arabic alphabet.

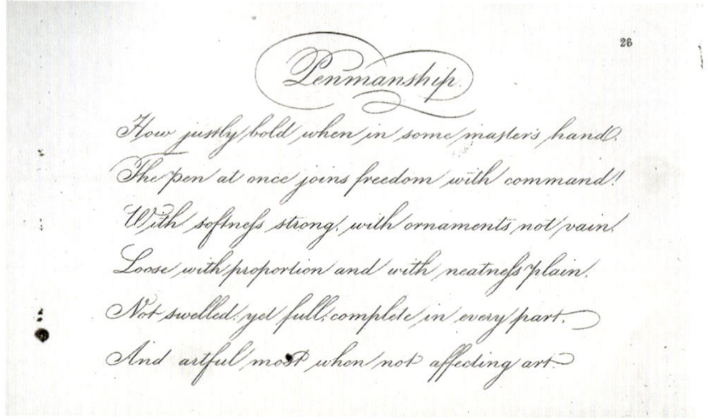

26

Penmanship

How justly bold, when in some master's hand!
The pen at once joins freedom with command!
With softness strong, with ornaments not vain;
Loose with proportion, and with neatness plain;
Not swelled, yet full, complete in every part,
And artful most when not affecting art.

Figure 7 Page from handwriting manual from the 1800s

The word in Figure 8 is an Arabic character decomposed on the right. Notice how the forms change depending on whether they are at the beginning, in the middle or at the end of the word.

Figure 8 Arabic word decomposed

DIGITIZING AND IMPROVING THE SCRIPTS

This is a special character called "fit right", designed to assist in drawing and spacing. (Figure 9)

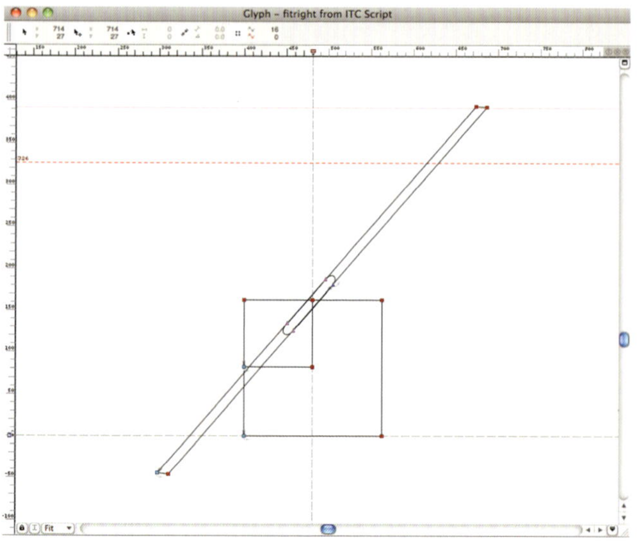

Figure 9 Fit right glyph

Figure 10 shows how the fit right glyph is used. Here is a grayed-out image of it in the mask layer of FontLab. It shows where to set the character width and the shape to end each character so that it joins with the next character smoothly.

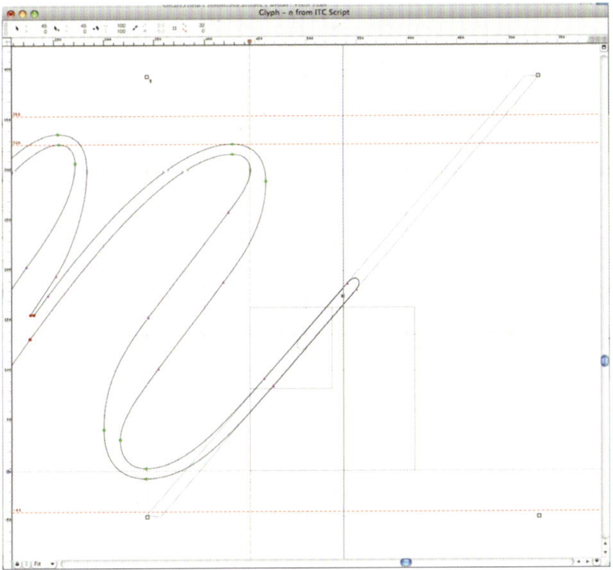

Figure 10 fit right glyph in use with n

Spring steel nib calligraphy is done with a pen nib that produces a thin line and with pressure the line gets thicker creating the "shadows" in the letters (Figure 12). The digital design was done differently. It had to be constructed on a computer in an outline form starting with a single stroke that was expanded to create the letter shapes. At first, letters were drawn with a single overlapping stroke. This ensured smooth pen-like shapes because they were made with the same principal as a pen. Scanned references were placed in the background layer as a guide for shapes.

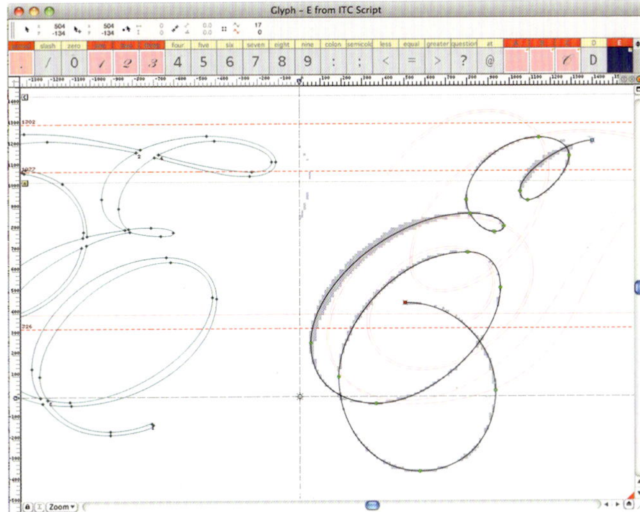

Figure 12 Digitizing step 1: single stroke line from scan

This is the spacing concept (Figure 11): where a glyph leaves off, the next one starts with an identical shape that overlaps.

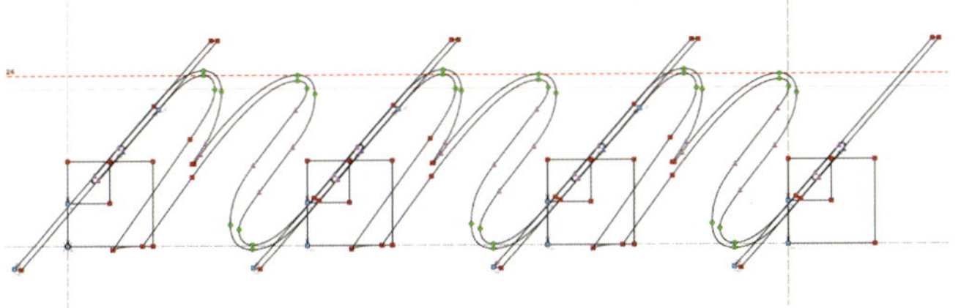

Figure 11 Spacing concept

The single outline was then "stroked" (technically expanded) to the thinnest weight with FontLab's expand stroke command. Expanded stroke shown on the left is the result. (Figure 13)

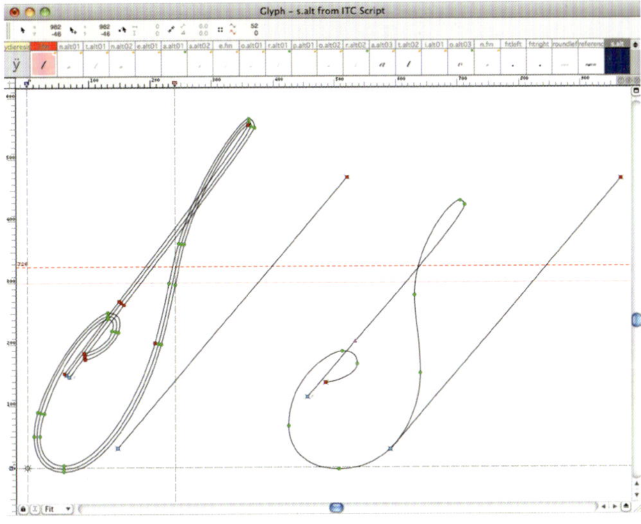

Figure 13 Digitizing step 2: expand stroke

Then the outline was drawn or moved around to add the weighted parts and other details, such as the joining overlap. (Figure 14)

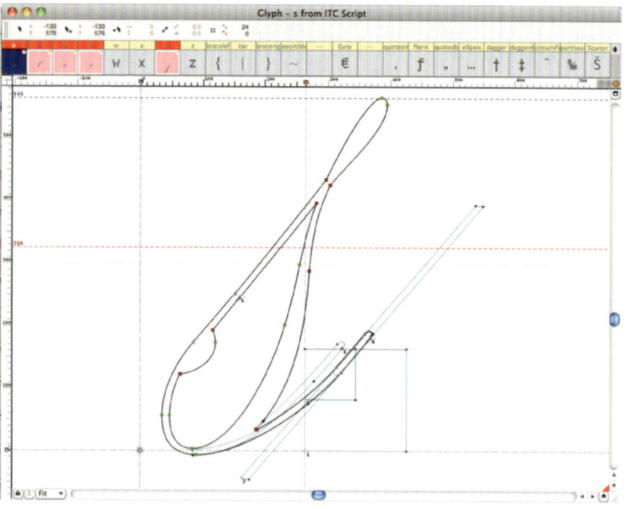

Figure 14 Digitizing step 3: adjust and draw details

Then the final shape was filled in and judged. (Figure 15)

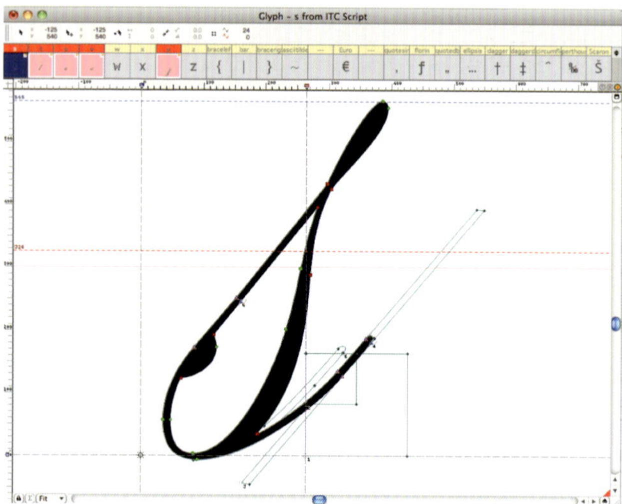

Figure15 Digitizing step 4: judge filled in shape

Elegy has varying weights in each glyph that were drawn to optically balance out overall when set in text. Some of the differences in weight from letter to letter. This is normal for spring steel pen lettering. (Figure 16)

Figure 16 Varying weights

Alignments vary as well as weights and were optically balanced radiating out from the center of the lowercase. (Figure 17)

Figure 17 varying alignments

Some of the typographic details from the original logo, like the half-circle loops in the o, give the Elegy typeface a modern look. This aspect of the design was retained and used for other letters that did not exist in the logo, such as the lowercase "s". (Figure 18)

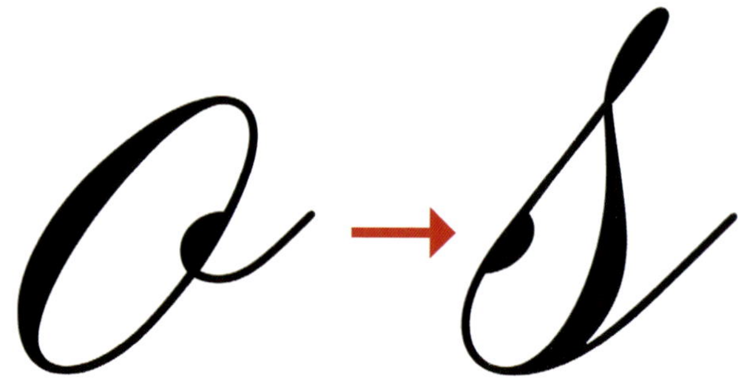

Figure 18 Design details in o and s

ADDING CONTEXTUAL DETAILS

Like Arabic, Elegy uses initial, medial and final forms. Here is an example of the three lowercase "e" forms: initial, medial and final. (Figure 19)

Figure 19 Initial, medial and final forms of e

OpenType contextual features are what make the font look like a convincing handwriting. (Figure 20)

Figure 20 Joseph's and Mary's sample of contextual substitution

The joins problem is also solved with OpenType contextual alternate substitution. (Figure 21)

Problems with joins without contextual alternate substitution

Better joins with OpenType contextual alternate substitution

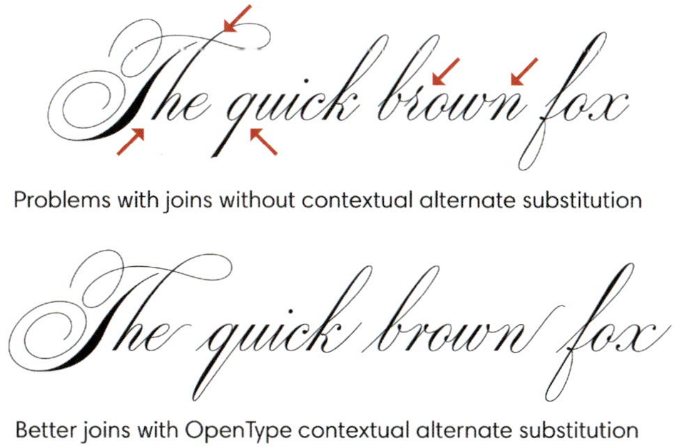

Figure 21 Quick brown fox sample of calt feature on and off

Two different shapes for lowercase "r" that automatically switch depending on context. (Figure 22)

Figure 22 Lowercase "r" in Fresh Flowers

DESIGNING ADDITIONAL CHARACTERS

The joining features are always "ON" by default. Some of the other OpenType features are off until the user turns them on, like "Stylistic Alternates". The old style figures above are stylistic alternates. (Figure 23)

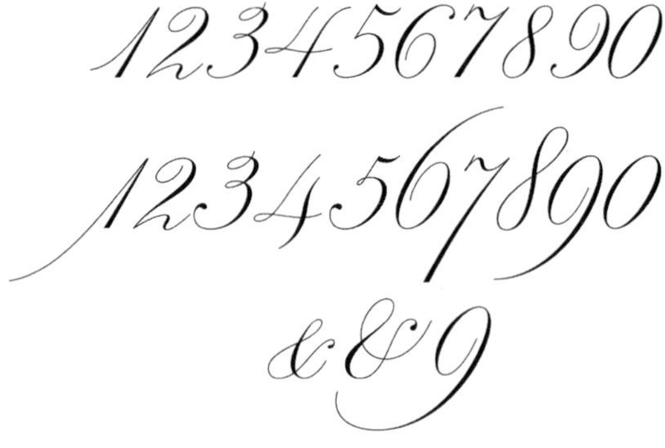

Figure 23 Old style figures and stylistic alternates

Alternate pilcrows were designed and are accessible through the stylistic sets feature. (Figure 24)

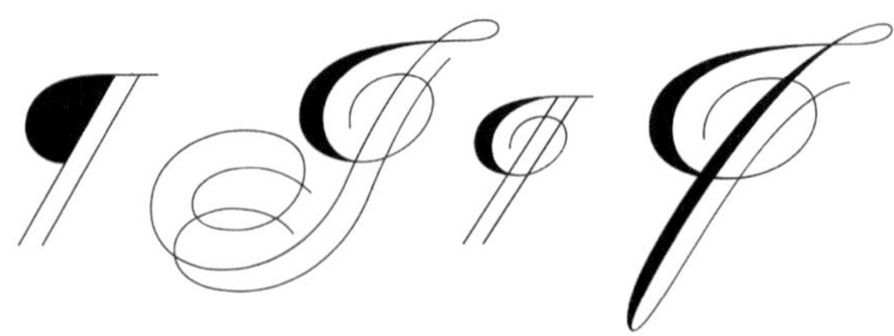

Figure 24 Pilcrow alternates

Elegy also has an "Arbitrary Fractions" feature. This enables the user to type any number with a forward slash, like 13/16, and get the complex fraction result like on the bottom. (Figure 25)

Figure 25 Arbitrary fractions

Ligatures and diphthongs were added to make some problematic letter pairs and joins more graceful. The stylistic alternates feature dramatically increased the number of glyphs to be designed. (Figure 26, 27)

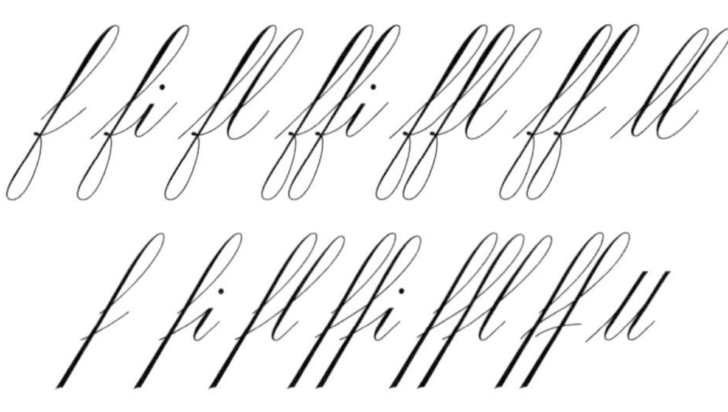

Figure 26 Ligatures

Figure 27 Diphthongs

Designing diacritics for Elegy was very challenging because all the sample references were in English – and did not include accented letters. (Figure 28)

Figure 28 Accented E, D, Eth, Oslash and Hbar

Monotype's European language experts in Germany, critiqued the design, and provided suggestion for improvement. Figure 29 shows a drawing Akira Kobayashi did on the right side with a suggested change to the Polish Islash that a native speaker recommended. With all of the different alternates for joins, and diacritics Elegy contains 1543 glyphs.

Figure 29 Falda Islash illustration by Akira Kobayashi

Elegy works great over a photograph. The letters are so thin and elegant that they do not detract from or block out too much of the image. (Figure 31)

Figure 31 Painting by Lon Wasco

APPLICATIONS

Used sparingly, Elegy can create logos by setting individual words. It can be effectively paired with a classic Roman type. When paring with other fonts, choose a lighter weight that doesn't overpower the thin strokes in Elegy. (Figure 30)

Figure 30 Sole Levante wine label

Elegy is naturally a good choice for wedding invitations and personalized note pads.
The ultimate sparse usage is, one letter as an ornamental drop cap. Here it is pared with ITC Berkeley Old Style. (Figure 32)

Seperation From Someone You Love
Is an illusion
In truth we cannot part
In my long to see you
I need look no farther
Than the depths of my own heart

Poem by Christopher Faris

Figure 32 Poem by Chris Faris

COMMERCIAL DESIGNERS'

Object of This Handbook

When using typefaces and fonts, users need to know some essential information and knowledge in advance, like font copyright, font licensing, and character encoding, etc. The ignorance of the basic information may bring about critical problems, even lawsuits; for example NBC Universal was sued for unauthorized usage of fonts. This feature is a handbook for designers' references when they are going to use fonts or typefaces.

Font Licensing

EULA: End-user License Agreement is a contract between the licensor and purchaser. In accordance with EULA, the purchaser can obtain the license or right to use the font software from the licensor. Legal font use is licensed, and only a valid license has obtained that one can use a font or font software on the computer. Purchasing a font actually means that one purchases a license rather than a software itself to use the software. EULAs vary with different suppliers and fonts and have different purposes. Thus, before using a font, one must read carefully every term of the EULA that restricts what one can and cannot do with the fonts.

Common Terms about Typeface

Font: A font is a particular size, width, weight and style of a typeface.
Typeface: A typeface which is also known as font family is a set of one or more fonts.
Font software: A font software is a "coded software that generates typeface designs when used with the appropriate hard and software plus any and all other data including documentation provided with such software".
Freeware fonts: Freeware fonts are fonts with no monetary cost.They are only free for personal, non-commercial use.
Bundled fonts: Bundled fonts are fonts bundled with software on your computer, which can be used provided the software is installed. These fonts are free to use on the computer and users should read and follow the license for other practical applications.
Shareware fonts: Shareware fonts generally are incomplete fonts, free for a short period of time before paying them.
Free commercial fonts: Free commercial fonts are fonts free for commercial use, with no limitations for time.
SIL Open Font License (OFL): The SIL Open Font License is a free software license which allows the licensed fonts to be used, studied, modified and redistributed freely as long as the resulting fonts remain under the Open Font License.

Intellectual Property Protection of Typefaces

Typefaces, fonts and characters are creative and intellectual property which is under the intellectual property protection of copyright, trademark, design patent law and agreement, etc.

A.Copyright

Copyright is a form of legal protection enacted by most governments to those who create original works with exclusive rights. Though the copyright system about typeface is the most commonly used type protection, there are still many difficulties and vagueness. The copyright status of typefaces is different from place to place because of various jurisdictions.

B.Trademark

According to the trademark protection, only the names of particular typefaces are protected. Thus the trademark system is the weakest form of typeface protection. If the name of a brand is trademarked, it means that this name is not allowed to be used by other brands.

C.Design Patent

A design patent is a form of legal concept to protect the ornamental design of a functional item. Typefaces, fonts and characters are protected by design patents in many countries. However, because of the cost and effort involved, design patent is the less popular type of typeface protection.

D.Vienna Agreement for the Protection of Typefaces and their International Deposit

It was initiated by some countries from Europe, such as Germany, France and Britain, and done at Vienna on June 12, 1973. The agreement claims that "The contracting states, desiring, in order to encourage the creation of typefaces, to provide an assertive protection thereof, conscious of the role with typefaces play in the dissemination of culture and of the special requirements which their protection must fulfill." This agreement will come into force once no less than 5 contracting states have been submitted the applications. Whereas, this agreement is still unimplemented since only 3 contracting states have submitted.

Encoding about Typeface

A. Character Encoding

Character encoding is a method of converting bytes into characters, which consists of a code that pairs each character from a given repertoire to facilitate the transmission of data through telecommunication networks or for data storage. There should be a character encoding system to display an HTML document.

B.Code Unit:

The code unit is a unit used for character encoding.

	code unit
US-ASCII	7 bits
UTF-8	8 bits
EBCDIC	8 bits
UTF-16	16 bits
UTF-32	32 bits

Font Formats of Different Browsers

Browser	Supported format
Internet Explorer	EOT
Mozilla browsers	OTF and TTF
Safari	OTF, TTF and SVG
Chrome	TTF and SVG
Mobile browers (like Safari on the iPad and iPhone)	SVG.

Useful Notes Before Using Typefaces or Fonts

1.Users should make sure that it is allowed to use the font since many fonts are sold commercially and cannot be used without being purchased from proper vendors.

2.Before using the font software, you should read the EULA (End User License Agreement) carefully. There are some restrict rules before you use the font. When in doubt, review the agreements carefully or get the explicit permission directly from the author.

3.The intellectual property protections of typefaces are different from country to country. The related information above is only for reference. If there is any confusion about it, please refer to the local laws and agreements.

INDEX

ACKNOWLEDGEMENTS

We would like to thank all the designers and contributors who have been involved in the production of this book; their contributions have been indispensable to its creation. We would also like to express our gratitude to all the producers for their invaluable opinions and assistance throughout this project. And to the many others whose names are not credited but have made specific input in this book, we thank you for your continuous support.

FUTURE COOPERATIONS: If you wish to participate in SendPoints' future projects and publications, please send your website or portfolio to editor01@sendpoints.cn

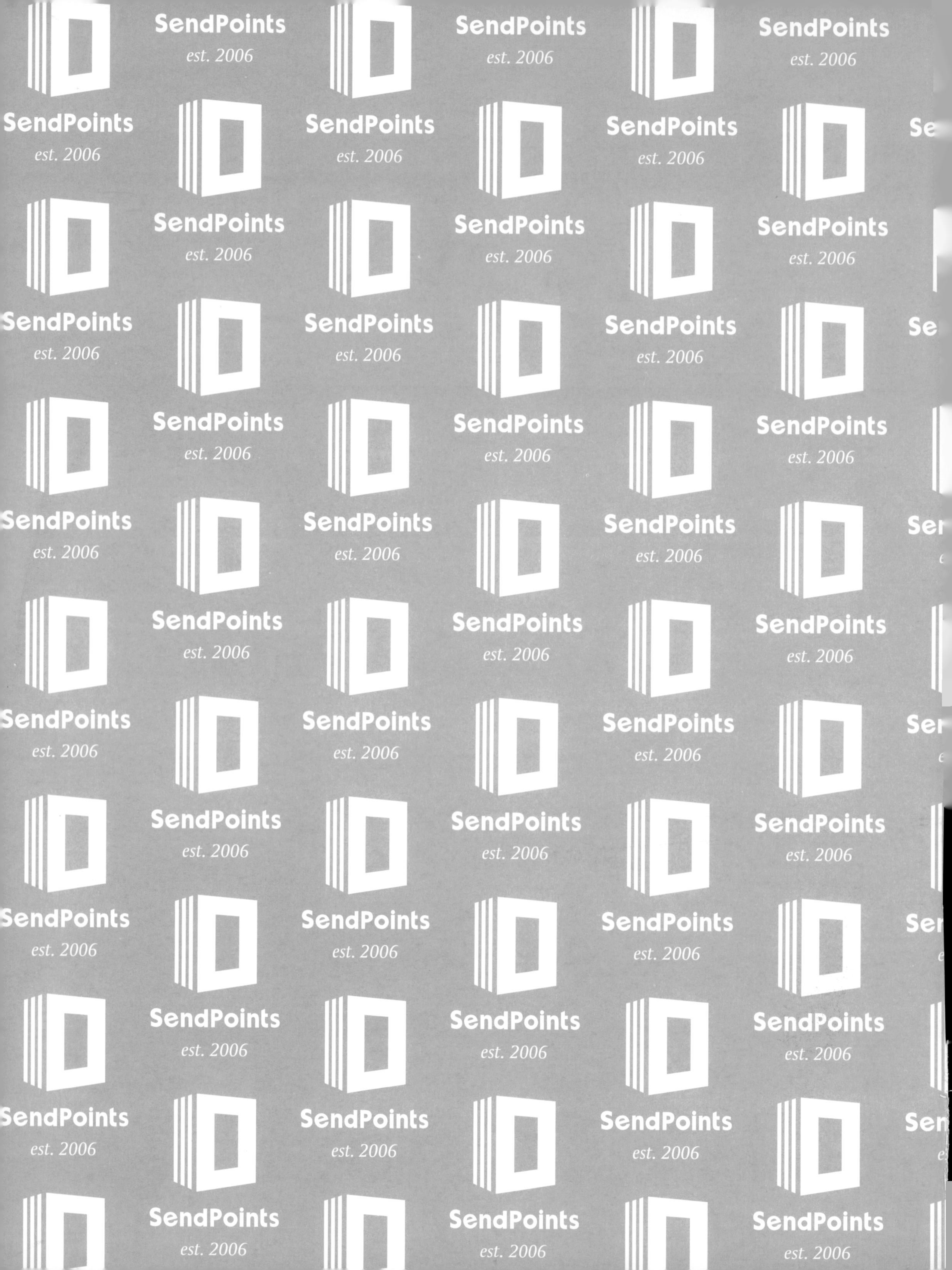
SendPoints
est. 2006